"*Christ's Girl* is uplifting, Christ-centered in every way, and full of both Amy's encouragements and Scripture. I believe this book is going to be so powerful for so many girls of all ages who struggle with who they are and need a gentle but important reminder that their faith in Jesus means they are indeed, Christ's girl. Amy has been in my life for years and her ministry has impacted my life and my own ministry now in huge ways. I am beyond excited that years of faithfulness to God in ministry to young women is being shown in a whole new way, this book! May God use this resource for His glory!"

— TALITHA PIPER MOORE

Co-Founder of The Dwelling, Daughter of John Piper

"With the voice of a friend over coffee, Amy shares gentle yet powerful truth the heart of every girl needs. This is an affirming book to not only read for yourself, but also to share with your friends, sisters, and every girl you want to encourage."

— HOLLEY GERTH

Wall Street Journal Bestselling Author of You're Already Amazing

"Amy's love for Jesus radiates beautifully through this book! In a clear and simple way, she calls girls to a deeper walk with Jesus Christ and helps them take practical steps to grow in their love for Him. As I read this book, I felt like I was sitting beside Amy, hearing her enthusiastic voice, seeing her radiant smile, and sensing her genuine care. Her love for Christ is contagious, inspiring others to desire that same intimacy and joy. I am excited to see other girls catch Amy's vision and pursue Jesus with all their heart!"

— SARAH MALLY HANCOCK

Founder of Bright Lights Ministries, Author of Speak Truth in Your Heart

"Amy's heart for the Lord and for girls to know Christ leaps off of every page. We have had the privilege to know Amy and see firsthand how the Gospel has gripped her heart. Girls who read this book will find in Amy an author who cares for them and, most importantly, the news of a God Who loves them to the uttermost!"

— PASTOR ANDREW AND HEATHER ROSS
Youth Pastor and Wife

"Some people speak well and others write well. Amy Vest Cox does both while modeling the message she shares in her own life. Her new book *Christ's Girl* is her testimony of living life in Christ. 'Let Jesus tell you who you are!' begins a book that is theologically-sound, Christ-centric, and Scripture-filled. We invited Amy to come to speak and then invited her back the next year because the girls (and women) responded to her truth-sharing, genuine, relational heart, and her face-to-face loving care. She writes, 'You will need Jesus, life in Him, and these realities every day for all of your life.' Indeed. May the Lord use this book to reach and disciple many of Christ's girls."

— JEANNIE BARGEN
Women's Ministries Director

"Amy has become the big sister I never had! The message she not only shares, but lives out, has impacted my life in the deepest way. It has inspired, transformed, and given me practical ways of how to live into the beautiful, thriving, all satisfying life we were created for! The love she carries, permeates throughout this message, which has led me to know and strive after the One Who loves me with my whole being, knowing a vibrant life is only found in the One Who created me."

— ISABELLA SWENSON
Mentee of Amy Vest Cox

"I will be forever grateful to the Lord for the invaluable influence Amy Vest Cox has had in my life. Amy's love for and devotion to Jesus Christ has compelled many young women, including myself, to know Jesus and walk with Him devotedly. As a young girl and into my teens, I eagerly anticipated Amy's conferences and girls' meetings because I so desired to grow in my understanding of God's will for me as His daughter. And I believe He, in a special way, has given Amy a gift for communicating to girls God's beautiful design for girlhood and womanhood. The wonderful truths in this book will encourage and enrich your heart because they are all drawn from God's timeless Word, which is sweeter than honey to the believer's soul."

— CARA DAUGS

Mentee of Amy Vest Cox

"When I went on this journey contained in the message of this book with Amy a teen girl, I had no idea what was in store, not even an inkling of how utterly and completely my life would change. The biggest thing I remember was the meaning, purpose, and value I began to see in my life for the very first time. I think of the verse that says, *"...He satisfies the longing soul..."* (Psalm 107:9) That's where all of this led me — to the feet of Jesus and the beautiful fulfillment and pure satisfaction found in Him alone. And that is what I hope and pray every girl finds as she reads these pages. *Christ's Girl* is not just another book on how to be a godly young woman. It is a much-needed message about what it truly means to belong to Christ."

— GRACE WILSON

Mentee of Amy Vest Cox

"This book is a must read for any preteen or teenage girl! It makes a wonderful personal study, but would also be impactful to use in a small group Bible study. I would encourage anyone working with youth to read this book. As a mom of 3 teenage daughters, I am so grateful to have this resource to share with my girls! Amy clearly explains the Gospel and the impact it can have on our lives. This book is for all ages and all maturity levels. Whether someone is hearing about Jesus for the first time or has been walking with Him for years, you will be encouraged and challenged by this book."

— SHARIE BLEVINS

Mother of 3 Girls

"As a mother of four daughters, I have always welcomed other godly women to come alongside my girls as we are instructed in Titus 2. Amy's mentoring teaching – similar to what is contained in this book – has been a form of that type of discipleship. Her encouraging, Biblical teaching has strengthened and equipped my daughters to love Scripture and their Savior – and to find their value and contentment in Him!"

— BONNIE DELAHUNT

Mother of 4 Girls

"Amy's voice is that of a friend running alongside you in a race. Grace effuses, spilling over each page, sparkling with an earnest appeal to know, pursue, and be transformed by Jesus. That which Heaven treasures, she beckons you to chase after with all the energies of your heart."

— STACY WOYTCKE

Songwriter of Precious Treasure

Christ's Girl

Experiencing Jesus and the Vibrant Life
You Were Created for in Him

BY AMY VEST COX

Christ's Girl

ISBN (print) 978-0-578-98658-6

ISBN (ebook) 978-0-578-98659-3

Cover Design by Annie Wesche

Cover Photos from Bigstock

Author Photo by Eric Vest Photography

Interior Layout Design by Sarah Lee Bryant

www.christsgirlministries.org

Dedicated

to my Jesus

&

to all of Christ's girls

*May you personally experience
the wonder of Jesus and the vibrant life
you were created for in Him as His girl!*

Contents

INTRODUCTION

Hi, friend!

I am so excited that you are reading this book! What you are about to read has the potential to change your life forever. You were made for a vibrant life in Christ and He has so much in store for you! The message in this book has changed my life and the lives of countless girls, and I know it can for you, too. I am so thrilled to get to cover this together!

I wish we could sit down face-to-face and talk heart-to-heart about this over hot chocolate and cookies! I am so grateful that we have this way to connect though, and I want to treat this like we are having a conversation in my living room or your favorite coffee shop. So, find a cozy place and open your heart. We can seek Jesus together. We are going to have such an amazing time with Him!

I encourage you to mark up your book — put stars by key points, take notes in the margins, mark favorite verses, etc. Make it yours, like a personal journal. It is about your journey with Jesus as His girl.

As you read, a study guide and an application point are provided in most chapters, for your help in embracing it. I really encourage you to do these. When you immediately apply it yourself, it brings so much fruit in your heart and life! There is also a "Focus Statement" included in each chapter to help you remember what you discovered!

You want this to not just be amazing information, but heart and life transformation. You want this to not just be a book you read, but a transforming journey with Jesus into experiencing Him and the life you were created for in Him as His girl. Right?

I am so excited to embark on this life-changing journey together! You were created to know Jesus and live vibrantly in Him as His girl. Nothing compares. Jesus is amazing – and He has amazing things in store! As you open your heart to Him and He meets you in the pages of this book, you will never be the same!

Are you ready? Let's go!

With love and excitement in Jesus,

Amy

P.S. While this book is written to young women, it also applies to "girls" of all ages. I will need these amazing truths for as long as I live, and so will you! All are invited to this journey of experiencing Jesus and the vibrant life you were created for in Him as His girl!

focus statement

The most important thing
in all of
the world
IS KNOWING CHRIST
& BEING HIS GIRL

CHAPTER 1

Catching the Vision

THE VIBRANT LIFE YOU WERE CREATED FOR IN JESUS AS HIS GIRL

"…Whom I created for my glory…" (Isaiah 43:7)

....

Do you know why you are alive?

Friend, lean in close. I have something very important to tell you.

> You were created to know Jesus and live a vibrant life in Him as His girl — a life where you are fulfilled in your relationship with Him, thrive in your Christian walk, and shine Him for His glory!

Stop and read that again.

This is why you are alive! This is what the Lord created you for, what He is calling you to, and it is where you will find your truest satisfaction!

Made for This

It can be so easy to think that life is to be born, grow up, go to school, graduate, get married, have kids, have grandkids, and then die. And that is often how life goes. But, you are made for a life that goes so much deeper. You are made for a vibrant life in Jesus as His girl, of knowing Jesus in a real way and experiencing the life He created you for in Him as His girl. It is a full and meaningful life that compares to nothing else. It is so real!

I am wondering, do you ever feel like there is meant to be more to life than what you are experiencing? I did. I came to trust Jesus Christ as my Savior as a girl and grew up in a Christian environment.

You were made for a vibrant life in Jesus as His girl.

Jesus changed my life. I loved Him because He died for me. I went to church and sometimes read the Bible. From this place of being His girl, it still felt like there was meant to be even more Jesus was calling me to in the Christian life than what I was experiencing.

The Lord was stirring in my heart, and He took me on an amazing journey with Him that left me exclaiming, "This is what I was created for!" I have watched the Lord transform my own life, and the lives of countless girls, through embracing Him and this life in Him. He can do it for you, too! Isn't that amazing? Let's jump in.

Why It Is So Important

Why is this so important? This is your purpose! Your spiritual life, living out of your life purpose, your heart satisfaction, and your eternal destiny, all hang on it. It is your true purpose, and you cannot be fulfilled unless you are living out your purpose. Do you see this?

It is essential that you know and embrace it for yourself. It is like a baby bird realizing that it was created to fly, and jumping from the tree, to experience the wonder of flight. Listen to what the Lord says, "...*everyone who is called by my name, whom I have created for my glory, whom I formed and made.*" (Isaiah 43:7)

"How do I glorify the Lord," you ask? You glorify the Lord as you know and experience Him and live the life you were created for in Him as His girl. It results in His glory, your joy, and being a blessing to others! This is what you are created for, and it brings inexpressible joy and passion to your whole life. It flows out in every area of your life in powerful ways.

How It Changes Your Life

It is so exciting! As you experience Jesus and the life in Him that you were created for, He will change your life in the most incredible ways. 1 Corinthians 2:9 tells us this beautiful truth: "...*What no eye has seen, nor ear heard, nor the heart of man imagined, what God has prepared for those who love him...*"

Look at this amazing reality!

Christ's girl is a girl who – because of Jesus – knows, loves, and lives in the transforming reality of:

⋙ Whose she is
⋙ Who He is
⋙ who she is in Him
⋙ what is true
⋙ what she is called to do

She lives in and from these realities by the power of His life in her through the Holy Spirit, for His glory.

Isn't that powerful?

Knowing the truth about what you are created for is good, but it is only when you actively take Jesus at His Word, believe it, own it, and walk in it for yourself – by the power of His life in you – that transformation will take place in your life. Like a baby taking a step and beginning to walk begins to experience the world – this changes your life!

A girl who becomes Christ's girl is one who responds to Jesus' call and comes to Jesus seeing her need for a Savior from her sins, places her faith in Him, receives Him and His forgiveness for herself, and turns from her sins to follow Him as His girl, by His grace. When she becomes His, she begins a life in and a relationship with Him, that she continues to grow in for all of her life until she enters eternity with Him!

Christ's girl is a girl who is alive in Jesus and living in and from the realities that are hers in Him by the power of His life in her. This changes her, how she lives her life, and the impact of her life on the world around her – from what she loves, to choices she makes, to how Jesus works and shines through her.

She is a girl who has Jesus and who He can grow in this incredible vision. She lives and puts her feet on the floor each morning, knowing in faith Whose she is and all of the realities that are hers in Jesus. She allows that to bring *This can be you!* purpose to and color all she does, from interacting with people to walking through her day, to doing work, to resting. Moment-by-moment, Jesus walks with her, transforms her, and works through her for His glory to make an eternal impact. She lives this vibrant life because of, with, by, and for Jesus – empowered by His life in her!

This can be you! I want this, don't you? Can you imagine how this would change your life? This is an incredible, purposeful life! Jesus said, "…*I came that they may have life and have it abundantly.*" (John 10:10) It is what you were made for. Such joy awaits you!

If you live as Christ's girl, here is a glimpse of the exciting results that you will personally experience:

❯❯ **life** – through salvation in Him

❯❯ **joy** – in Who He is, your relationship with Him, and satisfaction in His love for you

❯❯ **security** – in your identity in Christ

❯❯ **transformation** – from knowing and living in the reality of His Word

❯❯ **vibrancy** – from His life and work in you

❯❯ **strength** – as you are empowered by His life in you

❯❯ **purpose** – in following Him, fulfilling His call, and helping others know Him

❯❯ **impact** – for eternity as He lives, loves, and works through you to touch others for His glory

❯❯ **hope** – for eternity in Heaven with Him

❯❯ **and more!**

It is life-changing! You will see more fully how this connects to, and flows out of, your moment-by-moment life in exciting ways. It is what you were made for – and a life not to be missed! Are you starting to see a glimpse of the real purpose for your life? Let it draw you like the sparkle of a treasure in the distance until you experience Jesus and this life in Him for yourself! I hope this helps you see that nothing ever compares to this, and you go for it!

Experience It for Yourself

Have you received an invitation to a birthday party? You know about it and are aware of what's to come, but it is only when you respond to the invitation and go that you experience it for yourself, right? Jesus has given you an invitation to experience Himself, and this life available in Him! It is when you respond, receive it, and live in it that you experience it for yourself.

Ask yourself, "How would this change my life if I lived in Jesus and this life in Him as His girl?" Think about that for a second. How would it impact how you live, the way you think, and the joy you experience? Picture it in your own life. Powerful thought, isn't it?

Once you experience Jesus and this life in Him as His girl, you will never want anything else. It is like someone looking at pictures of the ocean, then experiencing the splendor of the ocean in person, and never being satisfied to only look at pictures again — except it is in a much deeper way. You want to experience it for yourself!

How You Live It

So how can I live in this? Let's look at it. You can be like someone who has the vision to climb a mountain, decides to climb, makes a plan, and begins the climb!

It starts with you looking to Jesus and His Word — the Bible — to see what you are made for. Then acknowledging a desire, and a drawing in your heart — for Him, His salvation, and the life you were made for in Him — that says, "I know I was made for Jesus and this life in Him!" Or, you ask Him to give you a desire if you do not have one.

Open your heart to Jesus and tell Him what is on your heart. It could be something like this, "Jesus, I need and want You, to be Yours, and to live this life in You! Please help me. I am all in!" Then seek to follow Him with all of your heart — by the power of His life in you!

He will do amazing things — and you will increasingly experience for yourself the life you were created for in Jesus as His girl! Psalm 16:11 tells this beautiful reality,

> *"You will show me the path of life, in your presence is fullness of joy, at your right hand, are pleasures forevermore."*

You can live it yourself! In the pages to come, we will look more closely at what it means for you to embrace and experience Jesus. You will discover the life in Him that you were created for as His girl.

14

Let's catch a glimpse of what we get to cover!

1. **Catching the Vision** – the vibrant life you were created for in Jesus as His girl (This chapter!)
2. **Becoming His Girl** – what it means to be Christ's girl and why it matters more than anything that you are His
3. **Walking with Jesus in a Real Way** – finding what your heart is longing for in a personal relationship with Christ
4. **Your True Identity in Jesus** – who you are because of Whose you are and how living in it changes your life
5. **A Girl of the Word** – the transforming power of God's Word vs. feelings, thoughts, lies, and culture
6. **Growing in Jesus** – the process of becoming like and radiating Jesus from the inside out
7. **Living as His Girl** – authentically living as Christ's girl by the power of His life in you
8. **Shining and Sharing Jesus** – sharing the One Who has changed your life with a world that needs Him
9. **Your Jesus Story** – your unique life story for His glory as you follow Jesus
10. **Your Personal Response** – your call to personally experience Jesus and the vibrant life you were created for in Him as His girl

This is going to be so exciting! Put on your seatbelt, because the Lord has amazing things in store for you! The most incredible life in Jesus that you were created for awaits you. It is when these realities connect with life, you walk in it, and you experience it for yourself that you are forever changed. As you begin to experience this for yourself, you too will exclaim, "This is what I was made for!"

(You can set the book down and jump for joy!)

For Your Whole Life

You will need Jesus, life in Him, and these realities every day for all of your life – at every age and stage. And you want it. There is no time like now to embrace it and begin experiencing it for yourself!

Do Not Settle for Less

Okay, let's get very serious for a second. So many girls miss out on this life that they were created for in Jesus – and experience the emptiness and heartache that results – because they do not understand their true purpose. They buy into the lies of culture, or they are held back in fear. The world, flesh, and the devil will try to stop you, distract you, and destroy you – and cause you to miss the reason you were created. Receive Jesus' grace, friend, and do not let them rob you of life in Jesus. The world and its ways may sparkle for a little while, but you will realize it is tinfoil compared to the diamonds of Jesus and the life you were made for in Him! Do not miss what you were created for.

Stop and think. What is one thing that is standing in the way of you experiencing this life? Is it fear, unbelief, small vision, people's opinions and visions for your life, or something else?

Write it here:

_____

_____

_____

_____

You will find that this is not worth standing in the way!

A girl who catches from Jesus this vision of the life He created her for in Him will not ultimately let anything stop her, as she lives empowered by His life in her. Right? She is like someone who has found a map showing treasure and how to get to it – who will keep the map in front of her until the treasure is hers. In the same way, keep the vision from His Word in front of you in faith, refusing to settle for less!

Yes, it will not always be easy. You will stumble and fall along the way, but the Lord will help you get back up and keep going. When you know your true purpose in Jesus, you will see that nothing else could ever compare with it. You cannot ever settle for anything less than Jesus and the life you were created for in Him. Receive the Lord's help and fight for it with all that you are – empowered by His grace. It is so worth it!

This Life is Real

This life of experiencing Jesus and what you were created for in Him as His girl is real! It is not a cute fairytale or empty actions you do. It is real, it works, and is transforming, fulfilling, and worth going after with all your heart! I have experienced it for myself, and so have countless girls. So can you!

Real for You

This life is for you, friend. Jesus is calling you to Himself, and this life in Him! It can – and must – be real for you! If you respond to Jesus' call to this life, you will experience it for yourself!

Insert your name here:

I, _____, was created to know Jesus and live a vibrant life in Him as His girl – a life where I am fulfilled in Him, thrive in my Christian walk, and shine Him for His glory!

It is as you personally become His girl through faith in Jesus as your Savior and Lord, believe His Word, and receive His grace to live in these realities, by the power of His life in you, that you will begin to experience this life for yourself — and you will be forever changed. Remember the sweet truth in 1 Corinthians 2:9: *"...What no eye has seen, nor ear heard, nor the heart of man imagined, what God has prepared for those who love him..."* There is nothing in this world like being His girl and living the life you were created for in Him! You can catch the vision and run after it with all of your heart!

A Call to Action

Will you personally embrace this life you were created for in Jesus?

Application Step

Stop and ask the Lord to meet you in these pages and help you know and experience Him and the life He created you for as His girl. You can pray what is on your heart. It could be something like:

> *"Dear Jesus, thank You for Who You are and this life that You created me for in You! Please help me to embrace You and this life with all of my heart! I want to be Your girl through salvation in You, desire to experience You and this life in You, and am all in! I am so excited about what You have in store! In Your name I pray, Amen."*

He will love to answer your prayer!

This is the life you were created for in Jesus as His girl. It is possible for you! It is what you were created for, called to, and where you will find the fulfillment to the longing in your heart! Are you ready?

Let's go! ≪

STUDY GUIDE

What was one thing that was especially helpful to you in this chapter?

_____

_____

_____

What is one step that you will take today to apply it to your own life?

_____

_____

What is one struggle that you face in this area that you can ask Jesus to help you overcome?

_____

_____

Look up these Bible verses and write what Jesus shows you:

• Isaiah 43:7

_____

_____

• Psalm 16:11

_____

_____

_____

- 1 Corinthians 2:9

_____

_____

_____

Pray or write out a prayer of response to Jesus.

_____

_____

_____

_____

Write the Focus Statement for this chapter.

_____

_____

_____

_____

You can write any additional thoughts here.

_____

_____

_____

_____

YOU BECOME

HIS OWN

through

Christ alone

CHAPTER 2

Becoming His Girl

**WHAT IT MEANS TO BE CHRIST'S GIRL
AND WHY IT MATTERS MORE THAN
ANYTHING THAT YOU ARE HIS**

"*...You are Christ's...*" (1 Corinthians 3:23)

....

What does it mean to be Christ's girl?

That is a powerful question – and it has an amazing answer!

Listen closely. Of all of the things that you will read in this book or hear in your lifetime, this is the most important thing. Your life and eternity hang on your response to it. It is so wonderful that it can take your breath away. Let's look at it.

> You were made to be Christ's, to know Him and walk
> with Him, and to glorify Him. Your sin has separated
> you from Him, but Jesus has made a way for you to

be His girl! Your life on earth and eternity depends on whether or not you are His. When you see your need for Jesus, trust Him as your Savior, and follow Him as your Lord – you become His girl, are right with God, and live with Him as His now and forever. As His girl, you can walk with Him and experience the life He created you for.

This is the most wonderful news of all! John 3:16 tells us, *"For God so loved the world, that he gave his only Son, that whoever believes in him should not perish but have eternal life."* It is far more than any happy news you hear from friends about exciting things – this is the most important news in all of life and eternity!

Why It is So Important

Why does it matter if you are His? You know the purpose you were created for as His girl. It all hangs on and begins with, this – being His. Just like a baby cannot experience learning to walk and talk unless it is born – so you cannot experience the life you were created for in Jesus until you are His! When you are His, you become spiritually alive in Him and this is all possible. It is the most amazing reality!

What It Means to Be His

What does it mean to be His girl?

As His girl, you personally:

⇒ believe in
⇒ receive
⇒ belong to

≫ follow

≫ are a disciple of…

Jesus!

Whether you are hearing this for the first or hundredth time, I encourage you to listen with all of your heart. This is so important!

The Gospel

You were created for a relationship with God that glorifies Him, satisfies you, and blesses others. Isn't that amazing?

But you have a problem. You have sinned (we all have), thought bad thoughts, done bad things, not done what you should do, etc.

"All have sinned and come short of the glory of God." (Romans 3:23)

God is holy, perfect, and cannot have sin in His presence. This means that your sin separates you from a relationship with God and destines you for eternity in hell apart from Him.

"The wages of sin is death, but the gift of God is eternal life in Jesus Christ our Lord." (Romans 6:23)

But the story does not end there.

God loved you so much that He sent His Son Jesus Christ to earth to live a perfect life, die on a cruel cross to take the punishment for your sins, and then rise to life again.

"For God so loved the world that He gave His only Son, that whoever believes in Him should not perish but have eternal life." (John 3:16)

Jesus calls you to come to Him as your Savior and Lord – and confess and turn from your sins to Him, place your trust in Him to save you, receive forgiveness and eternal life, and follow Him.

> *"...If you confess with your mouth that Jesus is Lord and believe in your heart that God raised him from the dead, you will be saved. For with the heart one believes and is justified, and with the mouth one confesses and is saved. For the Scripture says, 'Everyone who believes in him will not be put to shame.'"*
> (Romans 10:9-11)

Is that clear?

The Holy Spirit opens your understanding of your need for Jesus. Then, when you place your faith in Jesus alone for salvation; He gives you true and eternal life in Him. He cleanses you from your sins, makes you right with God, comes into your life, walks with you, empowers you to follow Him, and you will experience life in Him now and in Heaven for eternity! *"For by grace you have been saved through faith. And this is not your own doing; it is the gift of God, not a result of works, so that no one may boast."* (Ephesians 2:8-9)

Isn't this beautiful?

You have the amazing opportunity to see and experience this progression:

See your sin → realize the need for a Savior → understand the Gospel → place your faith in Jesus – become His, be forgiven, become spiritually alive, and receive eternal life → follow Jesus by His Life and Spirit in you → experience Jesus and the life you were created for in Him!

When you have come to Jesus Christ for salvation, He saves you, and you become a new creation in Christ, and a child of God – His girl! Then when God looks at you, He sees Jesus, His redeeming work in your life, and His righteousness! This is so breathtaking!

Imagine you were guilty of doing something wrong and were going to be punished – and a hero steps in, takes the punishment for you, saves your life, and makes you His. You would be so grateful, wouldn't you? Jesus is the greatest Rescuer of all time!

You see, becoming His girl is a call to follow Jesus – to be a disciple. You have the joy of following Him as your Lord and Savior! He is Savior and Lord. You are His. You follow and obey Him now. It is like giving Him the keys to the car of your life and saying, "Anything You want, Jesus, with me and my life – I am Yours!" Jesus Himself, and following Him, is not an add-on to your life, but you give your life to Him, and He becomes your life. This is what it means to follow Jesus. There is no one better to follow than Jesus! You do not want to follow yourself and your ways – it only ends in destruction. You were created to follow Him! True, eternal life is found only in Him!

When you have come to Jesus Christ for salvation, He saves you, and you become His girl!

Listen to what Jesus said, *"If anyone would come after me, let him deny himself and take up his cross and follow me. For whoever would save his life will lose it, but whoever loses his life for my sake will find it. For what will it profit a man if he gains the whole world and forfeits his soul? Or what shall a man give in return for his soul?"* (Matthew 16:24-26)

How to Become His Girl

"Oh, I want to become His!" Is this how your heart is responding? Becoming His takes place when you:

⫸ Come to God realizing that you are a sinner, your sin separates you from God, and you deserve to spend eternity in hell apart from God.

≫ See that Jesus Christ, the perfect Son of God, came to earth, lived a perfect life, and died on the cross to pay the penalty for your sins. He rose from the dead and stands ready to save you if you will confess your sins to God and turn to Him for forgiveness and life.

≫ Ask Jesus to cleanse you from your sins and be your Lord and Savior, put your total trust in His work for you on the Cross, and follow Him.

When you do this, He makes you His girl! It is like receiving a gift that you are being personally offered by Jesus. No one can receive it for you! If you receive it in faith, believing in Him, it is yours! I am sitting in a chair right now. I could just have said that I believe that this chair would hold me up, and I could know facts about the chair, but how did I prove I really, truly believed this chair would hold me up? By sitting in it, right? It is like this with faith in Jesus! It is not just knowing these truths about what Jesus has done and offers to you – it is also putting your full faith and trust in Him to save you. Realize that this is only where you will find true spiritual life, are truly alive, and will experience what you are made for – and the only life worth living! It is what matters more than anything in your life – or eternity.

Nothing is more important than this!

Will you receive it?

In Romans 10:9, the Lord promises, *"...if you confess with your mouth that Jesus is Lord and believe in your heart that God raised him from the dead, you will be saved."*

How to Become His

You can talk to Jesus right now! You can pray whatever is on your heart in response to the Gospel. You could pray something like this:

> "Jesus, I know that I am a sinner. I have sinned, and my sin separates me from You. Thank You that You died on the cross to pay the punishment that I deserved for my sins. I confess and turn from my sins to You, ask You to forgive me, save me, and come into my life, and I will follow You as Yours from this day forward."

If you prayed this in faith in Him, in response to His saving grace extended to you, and you know He helped you mean it – you are His girl!

"...You are Christ's..." (1 Corinthians 3:23)

Stop and soak in the wonder of that and thank Jesus for it. Nothing in the world is more important than this! This is your reality, now and forever!

What is True if You Are His

Let's look together at what is true about you as His girl! *"Therefore, if anyone is in Christ, he is a new creation. The old has passed away; behold, the new has come."* (2 Corinthians 5:17)

You:

⪢ are in Christ. This is your reality and position!

⪢ are spiritually alive. You are now alive spiritually in Jesus!

⪢ are right with God! *"Therefore, since we have been justified by faith, we have peace with God through our Lord Jesus Christ..."* (Romans 5:1)

⇶ are filled with His life by the Holy Spirit. Jesus comes and lives in you by His Spirit. The Holy Spirit comes to live within you — and empowers you to live the life you are created for and called to as His girl! "...*God's Spirit dwells in you...*" (1 Corinthians 3:16)

⇶ get to enjoy life with Him now. You get to walk with Jesus during your life on this earth!

⇶ will spend eternity with Him in Heaven. After this life is over, you will have all of eternity with Jesus in Heaven — your true home!

⇶ have a new identity. Your new identity is in Jesus and being His girl!

⇶ have an amazing calling. As His girl, you have a calling from your identity in Him!

⇶ have power to live out your purpose and calling. You have this power by Him living in and through you!

⇶ have a new family. Your new, truest family is all those who are His!

⇶ have an inheritance kept in Heaven for you! "...*An inheritance that is imperishable, undefiled, and unfading, kept in heaven for you...*" (1 Peter 1:4)

⇶ ...and so much more!

We will have the joy of looking into this more in the pages to come! Isn't this thrilling?

Your position is forever secure in Jesus. You are His and will be forever. No one or nothing can take that from you! No matter what happens in life, you can rest knowing you are His. Jesus said, "*I give them eternal life, and they will never perish, and no one will snatch them out of my hand.*" (John 10:28) From that secure place, you can live and grow in Him and experience the life He has created you for as His! It is so beautiful.

A Transformed Heart and Life

Jesus living in and through you brings transformation. It results in a transformed heart and life. It is life-changing and so incredible. You will see the fruit of Him and His work in your life! "...*Filled with the fruit of righteousness that comes through Jesus Christ, to the glory and praise of God.*" (Philippians 3:11) There are helpful ways to embrace thriving and growing in Him by His life in you. We will explore this more in the coming chapters. It is so exciting!

An Outward Declaration

As His own, Jesus calls you to baptism as an outward declaration to the world that you are His and you are following Him. Baptism does not save you, but it is an outward declaration that you have been saved and are following Jesus. It is a picture of you dying with Christ and being raised with Him to eternal newness of life. "...*Be baptized...*" (Acts 10:38) It is a privilege to declare to the world – "Jesus has saved me, I am His, and I am following Him!" I also encourage you to tell someone who cares about you, or who also loves Jesus, about you becoming His!

Some Serious Realities

The Truth shared above is the Good News – the greatest news you will ever hear in your whole life – about the Gospel, becoming His, and what is true about you when you become His. It is also really important that we take a moment and look at the bad news – which is not true for you if you are His. You must understand both!

What is True if You Are Not His

I am going to get serious for a second. This is too important to ignore – and I care about you too much to not give our full attention to it. Imagine for a moment that you were in a burning building.

You would want me to warn you, wouldn't you? Well, this is far more important than that!

You have sinned. This separates you from God and destines you to an eternity apart from Him in hell. This is serious, and it is a loving warning. I was in this place until someone told me the news about Jesus and the Gospel! I am forever grateful that they told me! This is who you are without Jesus: lost, sinful, spiritually dead, and headed for eternal destruction in hell, apart from God forever. If you are not His, this serious reality is true about you.

> *"And you, who were dead in your trespasses and the uncircumcision of your flesh, God made alive together with Him, having forgiven all our trespasses."* (Colossians 2:13)

I cannot overemphasize how important this is! You can be His, and the old realities, when you were not His, will be gone. If you are His, you are saved from hell, and in Jesus, you are saved, forgiven, and alive! There is no in-between. You are either His or you are not! If you are not His, you remain separated from God, and these things are still really true about you. Nothing else in this book – or in the life you were made for in Him – will be possible! Do you see how serious this is? When you are personally His, all the things He promised you are possible! You must be His.

Struggles You Might Face

There are things that seek to stand in the way and hold you back from the most important thing in life – becoming His girl!

They include:

> ⟫ **Trusting in your own actions.** Your good works cannot save you. The Bible says, *"By grace are you saved through faith, not of yourselves, it is the gift of God, not of works so that no one can boast."* (Ephesians 2:8-9)

and, *"All our righteousness are like filthy rags…"* (Isaiah 64:6) You cannot save yourself by your own efforts or good deeds. You can only run to the One Who can – Jesus!

⋙ **Your sin.** You could be holding onto, and loving, your sin more than Jesus. You can also wrongly think that you have sinned too badly or gone too far to come to Jesus now. Please hear this: no one is beyond the reach of His love and saving grace. No matter how deep your sin has been, His grace, forgiveness, love, and salvation are even deeper! You can come to Him and become His today.

⋙ **Caring about what people say.** You could be more concerned about what people say about you than what God says about you. This is so dangerous! Your salvation in Him, and relationship with Him, matter more than anything in this life or eternity! Do you see that clearly?

⋙ **Wanting to run your own life.** You could have false pride, believing you know better than God what is best for you. When you refuse to come to Jesus because you want to keep living how you want, it causes you to miss out on all He has for you and heads you for destruction.

⋙ **Doubts you experience.** You could be troubled by doubts about if He is real. 2 Timothy 2:13 gives this beautiful reality: *"…If we are faithless, he remains faithful– for he cannot deny himself."* You can also face doubts about whether or not you are truly saved. If you struggle with doubts about your salvation, you can ask Jesus for His help, look at the Gospel, and talk with a godly mentor or pastor!

⋙ **And, there could be other struggles that you are facing that are holding you back.**

Is there anything seeming to hold you back? If so, you can write it below:

_____

_____

_____

_____

_____

These are real struggles you may face. Jesus is bigger than them all. See that nothing is worth standing in the way, because nothing compares to, or matters more than being His girl. Can you see this? Ask Jesus for His help, and do not let anything hold you back from the most important thing in life and eternity!

What Matters Most

It is most important of all that you are His – and becoming His is the beginning of the incomparable life in Him! Listen to the promise of this verse: *"I have been crucified with Christ, nevertheless I live, yet, not I, but Christ lives in me. And the life I now live, I live by faith in the Son of God, who loved me and gave Himself for me."* (Galatians 2:20)

This relationship with Jesus, and life in Jesus, is only possible if you are His girl! If you are, you receive spiritual life and can experience this now and for eternity! It is like when you walk through a doorway into a wonderful place. When you enter by Jesus as the door for salvation – becoming His girl – it is the entrance into knowing Him and the life He has for you in Him! Jesus said, *"I am the door. If anyone enters by me, he will be saved…"* (John 10:9)

It is a Personal Thing

I personally heard and understood the Gospel, received Jesus, and trusted Him to save me – and He did! He has walked with me, kept me, and worked in me ever since. Other girls have personally known and experienced this, too. He will do the same for you, too! Is salvation in Jesus yours? Are you His, personally? Is it real for you? It is a personal thing.

Again, Romans 10:9 says, *"If you confess with your mouth that Jesus is Lord and believe in your heart that God raised Him from the dead, you will be saved."* It does not say, "if your parents," "if your pastor," etc. – it says, "if you!"

You must personally place your faith in Him as your Savior and Lord.

Just because something is in a flower shop does not make it a flower. In the same way, you going to church, being in a Christian family, knowing the right things, doing good things, etc. does not make you His. Your parents cannot believe for you. Your friends cannot rub their salvation off on you. Your pastor cannot save you. You must personally trust in Jesus as your own Lord and Savior. It must be something that takes place between you and Jesus.

Jesus is the only way to have spiritual life, be forgiven, and be made right with God. He said, *"I am the way, and the truth, and the life. No one comes to the Father except through me."* (John 14:6) You cannot get there by performing good deeds, through other religions, through your parents' faith. You can get there only through Jesus – the Son of God – the one God ordained to make a way for you to be right with Him, be His, and live the life you were created for in Him as His girl.

You must personally place your faith in Him as your Savior and

Lord, and it must be yours. When you do, and you become His, you begin life in Him and the amazing journey of experiencing Jesus and the life He created you for as His girl! Do you see how important this is?

Your Response to Jesus

It is your response to Jesus that is essential and makes you His! Will you be His today?

Application Step

Like we looked at above, you can pray what is on your heart in response to the Gospel. Or, this is an example of a prayer that you can pray:

> "Jesus, I know that I am a sinner, I have sinned, and my sin separates me from You. Thank You that You died on the cross to pay the punishment for my sins that I deserved. I confess and turn from my sins to You, ask You to forgive me, save me, and come into my life, and I will follow You as Yours from this day forward."

Again, if you prayed this in faith in Him, in response to His saving grace extended to you, and you know He helped you mean it – you are His girl! *"...You are Christ's..."* (1 Corinthians 3:23)

Welcome to being His girl, a life lived with Him, and eternal life! You are saved! That is the most important thing in all the world – and it is secure forever!

From this point, as His girl, you can walk with Him into the life He created you for in Him as His girl!

If It is Your Own

If it is your own and you have become His girl, you can fill in the spaces below.

"...You _____ are Christ's..."
(1 Corinthians 3:23)

You can write your name, and the date you became His, here:

Your Name: _____

Date:_____

This is what you were made for and there is nothing more important in all of life or eternity! ≪

STUDY GUIDE

What was one thing that was especially helpful to you in this chapter?

_____

_____

_____

What is one step that you will take today to apply it to your own life?

_____

_____

What is one struggle that you face in this area that you can ask Jesus to help you overcome?

_____

Look up these Bible verses and write what Jesus shows you:

• John 3:16

_____

_____

_____

• Matthew 16:24-26

_____

_____

_____

- 1 Corinthians 3:23

_____

_____

_____

Pray or write out a prayer of response to Jesus.

_____

_____

_____

_____

Write the Focus Statement for this chapter.

_____

_____

_____

_____

You can write any additional thoughts here.

_____

_____

_____

_____

Jesus
Christ
IS THE ONLY ONE
Who will truly satisfy

CHAPTER 3

Walking with Jesus in a Real Way

FINDING WHAT YOUR HEART IS LONGING FOR IN A PERSONAL RELATIONSHIP WITH CHRIST

"…He satisfies the longing soul…" (Psalm 107:9)

....

Do you know Jesus in a real way?

Stop and think about one of your best friends. You don't just know about her, do you? No, you really know her because you have a relationship with her as a person, right? You have spent time together, learned about each other, etc. – that is how you have grown to know and love her!

Jesus made you and wants you to have a relationship with Him that is like the one you have with your best friend – and even closer. What an incredible opportunity!

This is so amazing:

> When you come to Jesus and become His, it is just the beginning of a personal relationship with Him. From that wonderful place, He invites you to go deeper with Him, where you walk with and know Him in a real way – and He satisfies the greatest longings of your heart, transforms you, and overflows into every part of your life for His glory.

Isn't that fantastic? Jesus – the Savior and Lord of the universe – wants to have a personal relationship with you! This changed my life. It can change your life, too.

Can I share my Jesus story? When I became His girl, Jesus became real to me! I began to sense Him showing me that I was meant to have my own close and personal relationship with Him. I realized I was not meant to just to know about Him and pray every so often, but to have a real walk with Him moment by moment. As I received His grace to respond and follow Him, I made Him my priority and began really seeking to know Him and spend time with Him.

I came to know Jesus as far more than the One I heard about in church, read about in my Bible, or even prayed to – He became more and more real to me. I found what my heart had been longing for as I experienced Jesus for Who He really is, experienced His love, heard His voice, and saw Him real in my circumstances. I discovered that Jesus is the most important relationship I could ever have! He changed my life. Like Psalm 107:9 says, *"He satisfies the longing soul..."* I became more and more satisfied in Jesus and His love for me as I came to know His heart in a deeper way. I understood that I could trust Him in every area of my life. I was filled with purpose to live for Him and be pleasing and beautiful to Him – not because I had to, but because I then knew Him, and wanted to because I loved

Him! Since then, life has been an amazing journey with Jesus that I would not trade for anything!

You can experience Him for yourself, too! You were created for a close, personal relationship with Jesus, and it will change your life – you will never be the same! Second only to salvation, this is the most important part of the Christian walk as His girl – to be a girl who knows Jesus, is satisfied in Jesus, loves Jesus, and walks with Jesus in a real way. You were meant for this. He is truly real and will satisfy you. Jesus wants to be real to you! A personal relationship with Jesus is what you are longing for!

What a Relationship with Jesus Is

What is a personal relationship with Jesus? The word relationship is the key! What does a relationship mean? It means not just knowing about Him in your head but also experiencing and walking with Him in your heart and life. A relationship where you personally know, walk with, are satisfied in, and love Jesus in a real way.

Stop again and think about a good friend of yours. I have a really close friend – she is loving, kind, etc. How do I know this? Like I said before, I did not just hear or read about how nice she was. We have spent time together, talked, etc. We have a real, close relationship where I really know her – her heart, her personality, her likes and dislikes, and her life story.

A close, personal relationship with Jesus will change your life!

In a similar way, Jesus wants to be your very best friend, as well as your God and Savior. He wants you to walk with Him personally like you walk with your closest friend – and even closer! No other relationship will satisfy you as Jesus can. It is so key that you personally know Him. A close, personal relationship with Jesus will change your life!

Why Knowing Jesus is So Important

You were made to walk with Him, and that alone is where you will be satisfied. He died on the cross to end your separation from Him that was caused by sin so that you could be in a relationship with Him. He made you His so you could be in a relationship with Him. He is calling you to a personal relationship with Himself. Your whole life is impacted by where you are in your relationship with the Lord. As you walk with Him, your life will flow from your relationship with Jesus. Do you see how important it is? Jesus is the best and most essential relationship you can have in the world.

Why Jesus is the Most Important Relationship and Best Friend You Can Have

Here are some reasons that He is the most important relationship – and best friend – you could have – in addition to your Savior, Lord, and God! Starting to look at the reasons is like trying to count the stars though – there are infinitely more good things about Him. This is just a start! We will look at a few key reasons, and you can find more! (I encourage you to look up and read the verse references.)

- **He is the One you were created to walk with and glorify.** (Isaiah 43:1-3, 7)
- **He is the only One Who can save you.** That is the most important thing in all of life and eternity! (Acts 4:12)
- **He is a better friend than anyone else could be.** People are human and will have bad days, hurt you, etc. Jesus is the best friend you could have and He proved it by dying for you. (John 15:13)
- **He loves you more than anyone else ever could.** He loves you. Sit and soak that in. If you think about some-

one who loves you a lot and then multiply that by 100 billion-trillion, you start to get a glimpse of His love for you and the delight He takes in you! Listen to this verse, *"The LORD your God is in your midst, a mighty one who will save; he will rejoice over you with gladness; he will quiet you by his love; he will exult over you with loud singing."* (Zephaniah 3:17) Jesus loves you. (Jeremiah 31:3, Isaiah 62:5, Zephaniah 3:17)

≫≫ **He knows you inside and out.** He knows everything about you, even more than you know about yourself, and He understands you even when you cannot find words to express yourself to Him. (Psalm 139:1-6)

≫≫ **He is always with you and will never leave you.** People will fail you or leave you, but Jesus never will. He is with you every moment of your life! (Hebrews 13:5)

≫≫ **He is always the same.** He never changes and is the same amazing Jesus all of the time. (Hebrews 13:8)

≫≫ **He is perfect and the perfect example.** (John 13:15, 1 Peter 2:21)

≫≫ **He can transform you.** You cannot change yourself, but Jesus can transform your heart, mind, and life in amazing ways. (1 Corinthians 3:18)

≫≫ **He meets every need you have and you will find total fulfillment in your relationship with Him.** (Psalm 37:4)

There are so many more reasons why it is important – that you can discover – as you look into His Word!

Isn't He amazing? And isn't the relationship that you can have with Him such a treasure? This is the wonderful thing – the biggest call in your life as His is to receive His love and love Him! Jesus said that the greatest thing in life is to, *"Love the Lord your God with all your heart..."* (Mark 12:30). He made you this way and knows what is best for you! It is hard to love someone you do not know, right? It is so easy to love Him when He has saved you, and you personally know Him!

He wants you to experience these realities about Him in a real way through a relationship with Him! It is the most important relationship in the world!

Experiencing Jesus for Yourself

It is so vital that you know and experience Jesus for yourself! You can walk with Him like you walk with a friend — and in an even closer way because He is in you! You must know Him — not just know about Him — but to truly know Him. That is when your life will be forever changed.

Psalm 34:5 says, "…taste and see that the Lord is good…" It doesn't say just know that the Lord is good, or just say that the Lord is good, does it? No, it says "…taste and see that the Lord is good…" Do you like ice cream? Think about ice cream. (And try not to get hungry for it!) How do you know that you like it? You have tasted it, haven't you?

Imagine I was an interviewer on the street, and I walked up to you, put a microphone in front of your face, and asked you if you had ever tasted ice cream before. You answered, "Yes!" Then I asked, "Do you like it?" and you responded, "I love it!" If I then asked you to tell me three words to describe ice cream, what would you say? Think for a moment. Maybe you would say creamy, sweet, and cold or some other words to describe it, right?

So, picture this — You could hear how good ice cream is, have friends who love it, tour an ice cream factory, and even research and tell people facts about ice cream, but if you have never actually tasted it, you don't truly know. It is only once you have tasted it and seen for yourself — experienced it — that you will know for yourself. Your life will not be the same. You will want to tell people about ice cream and how wonderful it is!

It is *infinitely* more this way with Jesus! You can taste for yourself – know by experience – that He is good! You see for yourself that He is faithful, loving, kind, etc. As you come to know Jesus and Who He is, you will grow closer to Him and love Him more and more!

Let's look together at a glimpse of Who He is. As you read His Word, you will know more and more about Who He is, and then, as you walk with Him, you will have the joy of experiencing that reality in your life – and being changed forever!

It is so vital that you know and experience Jesus for yourself!

There is an endless list of Who Jesus is that you will have the joy of having your whole life and eternity to discover! Let's look at a few together – and then you can continue your own wonderful discovery!

Who Jesus is

- ➤ Loving – *"The Lord is… abounding in steadfast love."* (Psalm 145:8)
- ➤ Faithful – *"…The Lord is faithful…"* (2 Thessalonians 3:3)
- ➤ Forgiving – *"…You, O Lord, are… forgiving…"* (Psalm 86:5)
- ➤ Unchanging – *"Jesus Christ is the same yesterday and today and forever."* (Hebrews 13:8)
- ➤ Strong – *"…The Lord strong and mighty…"* (Psalm 24:8)
- ➤ Gracious – *"The Lord is gracious…"* (Psalm 145:8)
- ➤ Merciful – *"The Lord is… merciful…"* (Psalm 145:8)
- ➤ And so much more!

He is so amazing, isn't He?

What are some things that you know about Jesus? What are things you have personally experienced Him to be to you? List a few things about Who He is that you know for yourself here:

_____

_____

_____

_____

_____

_____

Look in the Bible to see Who He really is. (The book of John shows you Who He is, and the book of Psalms talks a lot about Who He is!) It is so important to make sure that you know the real Jesus, not just a picture other people have painted of Him.

Make a list of Who Jesus is – qualities about Him – and take time to worship Him for those things. For example, "Jesus, I worship You that You are faithful." Ask Him to be real to you in that quality of Who He is, and watch for it. Experience those realities for yourself. Your relationship with and love for Him will deepen.

The progression can go like this – you will:

read who Jesus is in the Bible → know it in your head → believe it in your heart → know Him for yourself → experience for yourself His goodness → your life is changed forever!

This is so wonderful!

How Knowing Jesus Changes Your Life

Knowing the Lord personally will transform your life!

Let's get a glimpse of how:

⋙ **He fills the longings of your heart.** The answer to the deep longings of your heart that nothing and no one else can fill are satisfied in Jesus! (Psalm 107:8-9)

⋙ **As you come to know Him, you can't help but love Him.** You become a girl in love with Jesus!

⋙ **All of the other areas of life will fall into place as you seek Him first.** (Matthew 6:33, Matthew 22:36-40)

⋙ **You desire to keep His commandments.** You love Him and know He calls you to what is best! (John 14:21)

⋙ **You become more and more like Him.** Knowing Him transforms you! (2 Corinthians 3:18)

⋙ **You look at life differently.** You see through the lens of Jesus and how He sees things!

⋙ **You are satisfied in Jesus, so now you have a passion to share Him with others and allow Him to touch them through you.** You want others to know the One Who has changed your life! (1 John 1:1-4)

⋙ **You receive a real vision and purpose in life.** A vision and purpose to know, follow, and share Jesus!

⋙ **You have the joy of living with Christ in this life and throughout all of eternity to come.**

We could talk about each of these – and more – for a long time, but you want to – and will – discover them by personal experience! This is your most important relationship, and you can really know Him in this way. Jesus will fully satisfy you and change your life!

When you personally know and experience Jesus in your own life, you cannot help but love Him and want to know Him more. Loving Him compels you to follow Him, obey Him, and desire to share Him. As you do, you get to know Him even better in the process, which makes you love Him more and want to know Him more – and the cycle continues! Isn't that so exciting?

Imagine – how could this change your life? How would your re-lationship with Jesus change what you think about, how you spend your time, and your actions? Think about that for a second.

If you pursue knowing Jesus in a real way, you will realize that nothing compares to knowing Him! Like Philippians 3:8 says, "...I count all things as loss compared to knowing Christ."

How to Grow in Knowing Jesus

You ask, "How can I grow in knowing Jesus?" Wonderful ques-tion! Let's look at some ways together.

Just like building a relationship with a friend takes time and in-vestment, so it is in your relationship with Jesus. There are powerful ways to grow in your relationship with Jesus – in knowing and walk-ing with Him!

Let's explore some of the main ways to grow in knowing Jesus. In other parts of the book, we will look at other exciting ways. As you do these things, remember it is a relationship you want to build. You are doing these things to grow in knowing Jesus!

These are ways to grow in your relationship with Jesus:

- **Ask Him for His help to grow in your relationship with Him and make Himself real to you.** Tell Him your desire to know Him! You can tell Him, "Jesus, I want to know You. Please be real to me. Please help me seek You." It is only as He works in your heart and opens your eyes that you come to know Him in a personal way. He loves to answer this prayer!

- **Make sure that you are His girl.** When you become His, it's the beginning of an amazing relationship with Jesus! You cannot have a relationship with Jesus until you are His. Make sure that you have come to the place where you have placed your faith in Jesus as your Savior and Lord and have become His girl!

⋙ **Make Him your #1 priority.** Jesus needs to come before anything else in your heart and then how you live your life. When He does, the rest of life fits into place. A real-life picture could be – You have some free time and are going to check to see if you have received any messages from friends. But you remember that you have not yet had time with Jesus or read His Word that day. At that moment, you have a choice of what is your #1 priority. Does that make sense?

⋙ **Spend personal time with Him.** Find time to meet with Jesus by yourself – with the goal to grow in your personal relationship with Him. In this time, you can: read His Word – the Bible, talk with, and listen to Him in prayer, record what He shows you in a journal, etc. Know that He is right there with you! So, your devotions could look like: going into your time acknowledging that Jesus is there with you, asking Him to meet you in your time together, opening the Bible and reading His Word written to you, responding to Him in prayer and worship, and writing down what He showed you. Your time with Jesus is just a springboard into a day of walking with Him! The more you spend time with Him, the more you will see the importance and joy of this time. *"You have said, 'Seek my face.' My heart says to you, 'Your face, LORD, do I seek.'"* (Psalm 27:8)

⋙ **Read the Bible – His Word to you.** The Bible is the Word of God, where you grow in knowing Who Jesus is, learn what is true, and see what His will is. I encourage you to read the Bible and ask Jesus, "Please help me to grow in knowing You, Your truth, and Your will for me more through Your Word today." The book of John in the Bible is a wonderful place to start – it tells you about the life of Jesus, Who He is, what He has done, and what He said. I encourage you to get your own Bible if you do not have one. It will be your most important possession! *"...The Scriptures... it is they that bear witness about me..."* (John 5:39) (We will dive more into the Bible in the *Girl of the Word* chapter!)

≫ **Talk with Jesus in prayer.** Prayer is so important! It is so vital that you talk with someone that you want to get to know better. Jesus calls you to come to Him in prayer. He is right there with you and wants to hear your heart. When you talk with Jesus in prayer, you can: share your heart with the Lord, worship Him for Who He is, praise Him for what He has done, confess and ask forgiveness for anything that He shows you in your life that is not pleasing to Him, ask for His help to obey, and listen to what He wants to say to you. Pray to Him like He is real, right there with you, and hears you – because He does! He hears and answers! *"...Pray without ceasing..."* (1 Thessalonians 5:17)

≫ **Walk with Him throughout the day.** Remember that the Lord is always right there with you. Walking with Him does not end when you leave your quiet time. You can share every moment and all of your life with Him! Every moment is an opportunity to know Him more.

≫ **Have special reminders of Him and His love.** This is fun and helpful in moment-to-moment life! When I was growing in Jesus, I wanted to have something that reminded me of Him, His love, and our relationship – just like I had special things that reminded me of specific friendships. He gave me hearts – anything shaped like a heart – as a reminder of His love for me.

I began to see hearts everywhere – a carrot slice in my salad, paint splats on the road, etc. It is powerful and helpful in pointing your heart to Him. So many times, I will be rushing along in my day, and He will bring to my attention something shaped like a heart that brings life back into focus.

One day, while I was cleaning the bathroom and having a hard day, I leaned over to scrub the counter, and there was a little puddle of water shaped like a heart! It was such a good reminder that Jesus loves me and that what truly mattered was Jesus and my relationship with Him.

Other girls who have wanted to grow in their relationship with Jesus have picked similar reminders for themselves. Realize that His love for you is real, no matter what, and these reminders are not necessary at all – it is just so sweet to have these reminders as extra help to turn your heart to Him. I encourage you to find something to have as a special reminder of Him, His love, and your relationship with Him!

> *Nothing and no one compares to, or can satisfy you, like Jesus can.*

Aren't these ways to know Jesus so amazing? They are tools to know your Jesus more. Let your own heart cry be, "...*That I may know Him...*" (Philippians 3:10) As you take the steps to seek Jesus through them, Jesus will become more and more real to you. Just like in a human relationship, the more you invest, the more you will know Him – and the better it will be!

I encourage you to take one of these steps today!

Which one will you choose?

Remember that relationships take time to grow. It is the same way with Jesus. Do not be discouraged if you do not instantly feel close to Him. As you invest in seeking to know Him, it will bear fruit in your relationship with Him over time. As you begin to know Jesus, your life will change forever, and you will want to know Him more. It is so exciting and worth it!

Application Point

Ask Jesus to be real to you and start with choosing one of the ways to grow in knowing Jesus to apply today!

Identifying and Removing Things that Hurt Your Relationship with Jesus

In seeking to know Jesus, it is essential to ask for His help to identify and remove things that hinder you in your pursuit to know Him. You do not want anything standing in the way of the most important relationship in your life!

You will struggle with many things that seek to hold you back as you seek to know and follow Jesus. Here we are going to focus on "love competitors." We will examine other hindrances in the coming chapters.

Jesus is the only One with the rightful place as first in your heart! Just like a bunch of children competing for the front of the line, so many things will compete for first place in your heart. We are going to call these love competitors – these can be bad things that pull you away from Jesus or good things that are being put in the first place before Jesus in your life.

Bad things – things that Jesus calls you not to do that are harmful to your relationship with Him – like friends who pull you away from Jesus, seeking for your own glory, etc.

Good things – things that are gifts from Him, but are being treated as more important than Him, and can never satisfy – like good friends, ministry, etc.

These love competitors can be:

>> self and reputation
>> friends and popularity
>> entertainment and movies
>> appearance and clothes
>> ministry and serving
>> distraction with boys
>> time online and on social media
>> money and possessions
>> skills and achievements
>> projects and work
>> wrong friends, movies, books, music, etc.
>> and more!

What are some love competitors that you personally face? Stop and ask the Lord to help you identify things that are holding you back from your relationship with Him. You can write them below.

_____

_____

_____

_____

You want to identify these things and see them for what they are – things pulling you away from Jesus! Then, ask Jesus for His help to remove those things or put them in the right priority order in your heart and life. He will love to help you. It is a daily choice. This will bring you joy!

It is when Jesus is in first place in your heart that you will experience the peace, satisfaction, and joy that you long for in your life. Anything else that you turn to besides Jesus for ultimate fulfillment will disappoint you and ultimately result in emptiness. It is like eating the wrapper for a piece of candy instead of the candy!

Psalm 107:9 is so true: *"He satisfies the longing soul, and the hungry soul He fills with good things."*

Nothing and no one compares to, or can satisfy you, like Jesus can. *"There is none like you… O Lord."* (Psalm 86:8) Do not let anything get in the way! Jesus is more wonderful than anything!

It is Your Turn to Experience a Relationship with Jesus for Yourself

Now it is your turn. Jesus is waiting for you with open arms. He wants to be real to you and have a relationship with you. He wants you to know Him and have a relationship with Him, and to satisfy you as a result. You will not be disappointed! You were made for this.

Jesus is inviting you to a personal relationship with Him.

The most important question in the whole Bible is where Jesus asks, *"…Who do you say I am?"* (Mark 8:29) Not, "Who does your pastor say I am? Who do your parents say I am? Who do your friends say I am? But, "Who do *you* say I am? Who have you known by experience I am?" Jesus is Who you are longing for, and a personal relationship with Him is what will satisfy you. Do not miss this gift of Him!

Jesus is inviting you to a personal relationship with Him. Life is amazing when you walk it with Jesus! Today you can begin to walk in a personal relationship with Jesus that is yours as His girl, that will continue until the day you see Him face-to-face and are with Him forever!

I encourage you to pause and tell Jesus your desire to know Him. You can say something like: "Jesus, I want to know You and grow in my relationship with You. Please be real to me." He wants to be real to you!

Will you answer His invitation to this?

As you do, your life will never be the same – and you will know Jesus and find the satisfaction that you were created for in a personal relationship with Him!

STUDY GUIDE

What was one thing that was especially helpful to you in this chapter?

_____

_____

_____

What is one step that you will take today to apply it to your own life?

_____

_____

What is one struggle that you face in this area that you can ask Jesus to help you overcome?

_____

_____

Look up these Bible verses and write what Jesus shows you:

* Psalm 107:9

_____

_____

_____

* Psalm 34:4

_____

_____

- Mark 12:30

_____

_____

_____

Pray or write out a prayer of response to Jesus.

_____

_____

_____

_____

Write the Focus Statement for this chapter.

_____

_____

_____

_____

You can write any additional thoughts here.

_____

_____

_____

_____

Your true identity

IS WHO YOU ARE

BECAUSE OF

Whose you are

CHAPTER 4

Your True Identity in Christ

WHO YOU ARE BECAUSE OF WHOSE YOU ARE AND HOW LIVING IN IT CHANGES YOUR LIFE

"Therefore, if anyone is in Christ, he is a new creation.
The old has passed away; behold, the new has come."
(2 Corinthians 5:17)

....

Who are you?

If someone asked you that question today, how would you answer? This is an issue of identity. Identity essentially means who you are – where you find your value or your sense of worth.

What would be the answer if you asked yourself, "Where do I find my sense of worth, security, and value?"

Listen to this priceless reality:

> Once you come to Jesus and are His, you receive your new, true identity forever. It is yours in Jesus, and it will never change. Every day you have the opportunity to increasingly live in and out of the reality of who you are in Jesus. The more you do this, the more your life will change, and you will experience more fully the life Jesus created you for as His girl.

Can you see how amazing this is?

It is so important that you understand this and live in the reality of it! It will change your life!

Stop for a moment and think of a princess. A princess does not always wear her crown, but she is still a princess, right? She still has to decide whether she will live in the reality of who she is. She can say

As Christ's girl, He has given you a new identity filled with realities that are true about you in Him!

— "I know that I am a princess, I know my father is the king, and I know who that means I am." — but she could still go begging in the streets, sit in the mud, and eat scraps from the garbage. Or, she can believe and live in the reality that she is a princess, and her father, the king, welcomes her into his presence. She can feast at his table, and all the riches of the kingdom are hers. She is a princess, but she must choose to live in the reality that she is a princess.

This is even more important for you as Christ's girl! You are His girl. He has given you a new identity filled with realities that are true about you in Him! If you know, believe, and live in the truth of who you are in Him as His girl, your life will be transformed. If you do not know, believe, and live in your true identity, you are still His and a daughter of the King of Kings. But you will not live in the spiritual fullness He created you for – for His great glory and your deep joy!

You can be like the princess and say, "I know I am in Christ, and I have heard who I am in Christ…" but go begging to the world for acceptance and to try to find your identity in the things of the world. Or, you can look to Jesus to learn who you are in Him, to understand your position and live in your true identity. Then you will experience more and more deeply the joy of living in who you are in Jesus!

You want to live in the reality of your true identity in Jesus! Look at this beautiful passage: *"But you are a chosen people, a royal priesthood, a holy nation, a people for God's own possession, to proclaim the virtues of Him who called you out of darkness into His marvelous light."* (1 Peter 2:9) Isn't that magnificent?

Let's dive into looking more closely at this exciting reality!

Let's Talk Identity

So, just to make sure it is clear, identity is who you are – where you find your sense of worth, belonging, or value.

You live in a world that tells you that your worth is found in how you look, what you do, how much you have, or how popular you are. This only leads to insecurity, fear, unfulfillment, and never measuring up, doesn't it?

You see, when you become Christ's girl, you are a new creation, and you have a new identity. 2 Corinthians 5:17 tells us, *"Therefore, if anyone is in Christ, he is a new creation. The old has passed away; behold, the new has come."* When you are His, then this identity is true of you. Your worth no longer lies in what you do, how you look, or who other people say you are. Your worth lies in Jesus Christ, what He has done for you, and who you are in Him!

This brings such freedom, security, and joy! Your identity is no longer you, but Jesus. Galatians 2:20 tells us, *"I have been crucified with Christ. It is no longer I who live, but Christ who lives in me. And the life I now live in the flesh I live by faith in the Son of God, who loved me and gave himself for me."* You see Who He is, and then you see who you are in light of Who He is!

Can you see how this is life-changing?

It is like a child who has been adopted. Suddenly, they are in the position of having parents, taking on their name, and receiving all that their parents bless them with – you are Christ's, and that suddenly changes your identity in the most transforming way!

It is so powerful! As you receive the Lord's grace to bring these awesome truths about who you are in Jesus from your head to your heart, and walk in the reality of who you are in Christ, it will change your life!

Why Knowing, Believing, and Living in Your True Identity is So Important

Why is this so important? Jesus made you His and gave you this identity! You were meant to know and live in it. It allows you to experience more of Jesus and the life you are created for in Him as His girl. That is what you want! Where you find your identity is so important because you behave in line with what you believe about who you are. Let that sink in.

The choices you make, your motivation for things, where you invest your time, your attitude towards life – all these flow out of what you truly believe about Who Jesus is and who you are, and they impact all of your life! Do you see how powerful that is? Let Jesus tell you who you are! Ask Him, "Jesus, who do You say I am?" and look in His Word for His answer. Listen to Him, believe Him, and live in that. It is so exciting!

Who You Are in Jesus

Who are you in Jesus? When you look in the Bible, you see who Jesus says you are in Him! Friend, this is who you really are in Jesus.

Jesus tells you that as His girl, you are:

≫ **A New Creation** – *"Therefore, if anyone is in Christ, he is a new creation. The old has passed away; behold, the new has come."* (2 Corinthians 5:17)

≫ **Forgiven** – *"…You…God made alive together with him, having forgiven us all our trespasses."* (Colossians 2:12-13)

≫ **Loved** – *"…I have loved you with an everlasting love…"* (Jeremiah 31:3)

≫ **Free** – *"For freedom Christ has set us free; stand firm therefore, and do not submit again to a yoke of slavery."* (Galatians 5:1)

≫ **Victorious** – *"…thanks be to God, who gives us the victory through our Lord Jesus Christ."* (1 Corinthians 15:57)

≫ **Child of God** – *"But as many as received Him, to them He gave the right to become children of God, to those who believe in His name."* (John 1:12)

≫ **Holy** – *"…Holy and without blame before Him…"* (Ephesians 1:4)

≫ **Complete** – *"For in Him dwells all the fullness of the Godhead bodily; and you are complete in Him, who is the head of all principality and power."* (Colossians 2:9-10)

≫ **Alive** – *"But God, being rich in mercy, because of His great love with which He loved us…made us alive together with Christ."* (Ephesians 2:4-5)

≫ **Accepted** – *"…To the praise of the glory of His grace, by which He made us accepted in the Beloved."* (Ephesians 1:6)

≫ **Redeemed** – *"He has delivered us from the power of darkness and conveyed us into the kingdom of the Son* *of His love, in whom we have redemption through His blood, the forgiveness of sins."* (Colossians 1:13-14)

Isn't this incredible? This is who you are in Jesus!

This is who you are because of Whose you are – Christ's! *"...You are Christ's..."* (1 Corinthians 3:23)

There are so many other realities of who you are in Jesus – this is just the beginning of the list! I encourage you to dig into the Bible further and find for yourself what the Lord says about who you are in Jesus. It is like a thrilling treasure hunt discovering who you are in Him! He has told you who you are in Him in the Bible, and you have the joy of listening and receiving it as true about you!

What is one aspect of your identity from the list above that means a lot to you? Write it and the verse that goes with it here.

_____

_____

_____

This is what is real about you in Jesus as His girl! Aren't you so grateful?

The Results of Living in Your Identity

Just like the princess living in the reality that she is a princess, as you walk in your identity in Jesus, there will be sweet results that come in your life!

Some of these include:

≫ **You see yourself more and more like Jesus sees you.**
As you look at the Bible – like looking through a glasses lens – you will see yourself as Jesus sees you, and it will have a huge impact! It is not how you see yourself, how

others see you, etc. See yourself as Jesus sees you, and let that change your view of yourself – and your world!

⋙ **You can be secure in any situation, knowing Whose you are and who Jesus says you are. Picture this in your own life** – you walk into a gathering, knowing who you truly are in Jesus and walk in that reality in that real-life situation. You can say, "I can walk through life knowing Jesus, that I am His, and who He says I am in Him!" Nothing can change any of those things! Isn't that beautiful?

⋙ **You can focus on Jesus alone and what He thinks of you, and you do not need to face emotional ups and downs based on worrying about what people think of you.** Instead, you can rest in what He has said about who you are.

⋙ **You are transformed as you know and live more and more in and from your true identity**.

As you grow in your understanding of your true identity in Jesus and increasingly live a life matching your position, you will be transformed. You will live more and more in daily life what is true about you spiritually. So, you live more loved, free, redeemed, etc.!

⋙ **You have joy as you experience the reality of your true identity in your life.** As you experience the reality of your identity in real life, it brings you so much joy.

⋙ **The Lord is glorified.** Through your life, it will be seen how amazing He is as He gives, shows, and helps you to live in and experience the joy of your real identity in Him!

These things will lead you into a deeper relationship with Him and love for Him – and will allow Him to work more freely through you.

Can you see how it would change your life? It is so exciting!

Personal Transformation

I have found the power of this in my own life – and so can you!

As you receive the Lord's grace to walk day-to-day in the reality of who you are in Jesus, you are increasingly able to live and walk into any setting and rest in and be confident in who you are in Jesus. Whether people love you or hate you, or think you are wonderful or weird, you can be at peace knowing your position in Christ and what He thinks of you. You can walk into church, a social gathering, or anywhere at all, and not need to look around at everyone and hope they accept you – you can be confident of, and secure in, who you are in Christ and be able to shine His love!

Every day of my life, I need to walk in the reality of who I am in Jesus! Understanding who I am because of Jesus and what He has done continues to grow my gratitude for Jesus and be life-altering for me. When I am not living in the reality of my identity in Jesus, I find I become insecure. But, when Jesus directs my eyes back to my position in Him and my value because of Him, the security in Him returns! I want to live more fully in my identity in Christ with each breath I take.

This is something you want, isn't it? Oh yes!

How to Live in Your True Identity

How do you live in your identity?

Let's take a look!

Look to Jesus in His Word to see who you are, listen to Him, believe Him, live in and from the reality of who you are in Jesus – and experience the results! As you live and rest in your true identity in Christ, it will bring you freedom to pursue what God has for you.

Living out your identity in Jesus is a beautiful process:

⋙ Listen to Him in His Word – the Bible.

⋙ Know who you are.

⋙ Believe Him.

⋙ Live in that reality.

⋙ Live from that reality.

⋙ Experience the transformation that results.

It is thrilling!

Listen to Ephesians 5:8: *"…For at one time you were darkness, but now you are light in the Lord. Walk as children of light…"* It is a reminder of who you are and a call to walk in the reality of who you are! Live as who you are.

You receive your true identity in Jesus forever. It will not change. But every day, you have the opportunity to live more and more in and out of the reality of who you are in Jesus.

Let's get really practical and picture this in real life!

For example, as you seek to live in and from your true identity, you can say:

"If I believe I am _____, with the Lord's help, I will _____ _____."

Here are some examples:

⋙ "If I believe I am loved, I will not desperately seek for love from other places that will not fully satisfy."

⋙ "If I believe I am accepted, I will not do things to try to earn the acceptance of others – which can lead to so much trouble."

⋙ "If I believe I am victorious, I will not accept the defeat the enemy wants to bring in an area of sin in my life."

Fill in a couple for yourself:

> "If I believe I am _____, with
> the Lord's help, I will _____
> _____."
>
> "If I believe I am _____, with
> the Lord's help, I will _____
> _____."

Do you get the idea? Isn't that so exciting?

Watch how it changes you! It will transform your life!

Identity changes how you live. You can look at yourself in the mirror in the morning and see a girl who is loved, forgiven, and free in Jesus. And you can head out the door, knowing – and humbly confident in – who you are in Jesus – and walk through the day in that reality! Isn't that an incredible thought?

It is a life-long process of growing in walking more fully in your identity in Christ. You will become in practice who you are already in your position. It is knowing you are unchangeably accepted and receiving God's grace to grow in living like it!

Stop and look at your life, and ask yourself for real, "Where am I finding my identity?" This is helpful to do every day.

Choose to find your identity in Christ!

Identity Implies a Call

When you know who you are, then you know how you are called to live. Someone who is in the position of an ambassador for a country has the call to represent their country to other countries. In a similar way, your identity – your position and who you are in Jesus

– holds a call to live from that reality. And the beautiful thing is, you already have that identity, and His Spirit is empowering you to live from and fulfill what He has called you to! For example, Jesus tells you, *"You are the light of the world..."* (Matthew 5:14) and what your call is, *"...let your light shine..."* (Matthew 5:16) We will look at how you can live out this call aspect in other practical ways in some of the chapters to come! So exciting, isn't it?

You Live from Your Identity and Not for It

Remember, you live from your identity in Jesus, not to earn or keep it. You are not living for, or to receive, or keep an identity – you are living from a secure identity. You are not trying to earn God's favor or salvation – or people's acceptance and validation – as a means of worth and identity. Instead, you have the acceptance and validation you need in Jesus – and you can live from it to glorify Him and bless others as an outflow! This truth is freeing and empowering as you live from love for Jesus, instead of it being exhausting and impossible. This difference is so important!

Jesus alone has the right to define you.

Struggles You Will Face

Friend, hear this, Jesus is the only One Who has the right to define you! He is the One Who created you and saved you.

Like we have already seen, when Jesus has His amazing way for you in something, there will be lots of other options that are competing for that place – but these rivals only bring sad results. You will be tempted and can naturally tend to look for your identity, worth, and security in all kinds of places other than Jesus. So many other things will try to define you – culture, feelings, what other people say, what you have done, your sin, thoughts, etc. Don't turn to someone or something else to define you or tell you who you are. Jesus has already told you who you are – you just need to listen to Him and not to yourself or the voices of others! Jesus alone has the right to define you – through Who He is, what He has done, who He made you to be, and who He says you are in Him.

Let's look at some places that you could be tempted to look for false identity.

False Identities

Beware of false identities!

A false identity is finding your sense of worth, value, or importance in something other than Jesus and who you are in Him.

Some false identities include:

>> what people say, have said, or might say about you

>> what you have or have not done

>> what has happened or been done to you

>> how you look or your clothes or the image you portray online

>> your talents or personality or intelligence

>> your achievements and performance in school, sports, work, etc.

>> your possessions and money

>> your hobbies or entertainment

>> your health and food

>> your friends and popularity

>> your family or relationship status

>> your being a good girl or having godly standards

>> your service for God or good works

What are some false identities that you personally face?

_____

_____

_____

Your source of worth is meant to go so much deeper than these things. Your worth does not depend on the brand of clothes you wear, who your friends are, or the things that you can do well!

Consider if your identity is in how well you can play a sport and then you have an injury making it impossible to play that sport again? Or, if your identity is in your friends and they turn their backs on you? Or, if your identity is in your belongings and they get stolen? Then your foundation for your identity is gone, right?

You are not the clothes you wear, your social media image, or how well you can do a skill – you are who Jesus says you are in Him. This identity in Jesus is unshakeable!

Find your identity alone in Jesus and who He says you are. This is your true identity!

A Few Struggle Areas

⋙ **You are not what you feel or think.** Feelings and thoughts come and go, and they go up and down. We know that as girls, don't we? Do not believe them. You cannot trust them or let them define you! Only Jesus can do that! You can confidently say, "I may feel this way _____ (how you feel), but I know that _____ (your identity) is who I really am!" "...For whenever our heart condemns us, God is greater than our heart, and he knows everything." (1 John 3:2)

➤ **You are not who people say you are.** It can be easy to receive your identity from the things that you can see and the things people praise you for, like: "You are so good at music!" or "I love your hair!" or "You always wear cute clothes!" or "You are such a helper!" You can even draw your sense of identity from things they say about you unkindly, like: "You are not very smart!" or "You are ugly." or "You are a failure!" People have no right to define you. Only Jesus – the One Who made you and saved you has this right!

Let's think about labels for a moment. Have you ever looked at the labels on a jar? Imagine a jar of delicious strawberry jam. Someone could accidentally – or purposefully – put a label on that jar that says it contains lima beans or tuna fish. But, that does not change what it truly is – what is inside – does it? It is still strawberry jam!

People will try to put labels on you all of the time. Labels telling you who you are. Those labels are often misleading or wrong – and those labels from people can be peeled off. Jesus tells you who you truly are in Him. The more you believe and live in what He says, the less the labels from people (good or bad) will affect you. What are some labels people have put on you? Do they echo Jesus and match with what He says about you, or not? Listen to Jesus!

➤ **Your circumstances do not define you.** God can use them to grow you in Him, but they do not define you. You may be in a season where things are going very well or in a very hard season. Neither one defines you. Or, for example, you may be battling a long-term illness. No matter the circumstances, you are defined by Jesus and not your illness.

≫ **You are not what you do or do not do.** Those are an outflow of what is in your heart, but they do not define you. They are what you do, not who you are.

≫ **You are not who the enemy – the devil – says you are.** The devil will try to tell you that you are defined by your past mistakes, your current shortcomings, or some other flat-out lie. The Bible tells us the devil is, *"…the accuser…"* (Revelation 12:10). He will try to make you feel condemned when Jesus has already told you, *"There is therefore now no condemnation for those who are in Christ Jesus."* (Romans 8:1) When you are tempted to believe the devil's accusations and lies, look to Jesus, remember He has overcome the devil, and what He says is true.

≫ **Your struggles do not define you.** They are what you struggle with and not who you are. For example, say you struggle with anxiety. You are a beloved daughter of the King who struggles with anxiety and who has a Savior Who covered that anxiety with His blood and will give you grace – as you face that anxiety – to press into Him. You are not an anxious person. It is a struggle you face, not who you are. I have struggled with thinking that my feelings define me. This causes so much insecurity and instability. Feelings can be all over the place, can't they? When I rest in Jesus defining me and who He says I am in Him, it results in so much peace and stability. It gives me security even when my feelings are all over the place. I am so grateful!

Ask, "Jesus, who do You say I am?" Look at His Word, receive the answer, believe Him, and live in that!

Lean in close and really get this – you are who Jesus says you are – no matter what other people say, how you feel, or the way culture defines you.

You see, an identity based on you, your performance, what you own, what you can do well, how people think of you, etc., will lead you into an identity crisis – because those things will fail, disappoint you, and never fully fulfill. An identity based on Jesus will bring you the security, meaning, and purpose you long for because Jesus never fails you. He tells you who you are forever in Him, and He alone can totally fulfill you!

Again, listen to and believe Jesus. He has told you who you are in His Word. Ask, "Jesus, who do You say I am? What do You say about me?" He has told you amazing, life-changing things about who you are in Him. Look at His Word, receive the answer, believe Him, and live in that!

Yes, find your identity in Jesus and who He says you are in Him alone!

Beautiful Truths

It is so powerful to remind yourself of these beautiful truths that are yours when you are in Christ:

- ⟫ You are not defined by your worst day, what you have done, or what you do – but by what Jesus has done for you and who He has made you!
- ⟫ You are not defined by how you look, but by what God sees when He looks at you – He sees Jesus!
- ⟫ You are not defined by what you have accomplished, but by what Jesus has accomplished for you on the Cross!
- ⟫ You are not defined by what you know, or even the fact that you know God, but by the fact that God knows you because of Jesus!

⋙ You are not defined by what people say about you, but by what God says about you!

⋙ You are not defined by who you are in yourself, but by Who Jesus is in you and who He has made you in Him!

You can stop and thank Jesus for this!

Rest in the Reality

You can rest in the beauty of your identity in Jesus. This is who He has made you because you are His. Soak in that reality like the warmth of the sunshine on your skin. It is yours in Jesus.

I want you to look at this beautiful Bible passage that talks so much about who you are in Jesus!

*"Blessed be the God and Father of our Lord Jesus Christ, who has **blessed** us in Christ **with every spiritual blessing** in the heavenly places, even as he chose us in him before the foundation of the world, that we should be **holy** and **blameless** before him. In love he predestined us for **adoption** to himself as sons through Jesus Christ, according to the purpose of his will, to the praise of his glorious grace, with which he has blessed us in the Beloved. **In him** we have **redemption** through his blood, the **forgiveness** of our trespasses, according to the riches of his grace…"* (Ephesians 1:3-7, emphasis added)

Oh, what an incredible treasure you have as Christ's girl! Isn't it amazing the gift that is yours in your true identity in Jesus?

One Step to Embrace It

I want to encourage you to take this one step towards knowing and living in your identity in Jesus! You will be so blessed as you do!

Write out one reality of your identity in Jesus that your heart especially needs right now and a Bible verse about it on a card. Put it somewhere you will see it often – like by your bed, on the mirror, in your bag, etc. This will remind you often of who you are in Jesus! Soak in and seek to live from this reality by His powerful grace available to you by the Holy Spirit living within you.

For example:

I am loved

"...I have loved you with an everlasting love..."
(Jeremiah 31:3)

You can put the cards up all around your room where you see them and are reminded of them. You will find incredible results as you are reminded of this truth each day!

Go Live in Your Identity

Friend, you have seen life-changing truths about your identity in Jesus. This is your true identity if you are His girl through salvation. Jesus meant for you to know, believe, and live in this reality! Understanding and living in your identity in Jesus will transform your life.

Understanding and living in your identity in Jesus will transform your life.

Keep looking to Jesus and His Word for a definition of your true identity, choose to find your worth and value in Christ, live daily in the reality, hope, freedom, and security of who you are in Him, and watch Him transform your life! You will experience more of what He created and redeemed you for. This will cause you to increasingly love and worship Jesus – and fulfill your life's purpose!

Pause and thank Jesus for your true identity in Him and ask Him to help you walk in your identity in Him. You could pray something like: "Jesus, thank You for who I am in You. Please help me to live in its reality!"

This is who you are because of Whose you are. Know your true identity, believe it, and walk in it. Jesus will do amazing things as you do! It is so exciting!

Go and live in your true identity in Christ! ≪

STUDY GUIDE

What was one thing that was especially helpful to you in this chapter?

_____

_____

_____

What is one step that you will take today to apply it to your own life?

_____

_____

What is one struggle that you face in this area that you can ask Jesus to help you overcome?

_____

_____

Look up these Bible verses and write what Jesus shows you:

*   2 Corinthians 5:17

_____

_____

*   Colossians 1:13-14

_____

_____

- Colossians 2:12-13

_____

_____

_____

_____

Pray or write out a prayer of response to Jesus.

_____

_____

_____

_____

Write the Focus Statement for this chapter.

_____

_____

_____

You can write any additional thoughts here.

_____

_____

_____

_____

THE BIBLE IS NOT

JUST MEANT TO

inform you

BUT TO

transform you

CHAPTER 5

A Girl of the Word

THE TRANSFORMING POWER OF GOD'S WORD VS. FEELINGS, THOUGHTS, LIES & CULTURE

"…If you abide in my word, you are truly my disciples, and you will know the truth, and the truth will set you free."
(John 8:31-32)

....

Who — or what — do you believe?

Imagine that your best friend sent you a message. You would open it right away and devour its contents, wouldn't you? This is what the Bible is – the Lord's message to you!

Friend, wrap your mind around this reality:

The Bible is the Word of God to you. Through it you come to know Him, what is true, who you are in Him, what you are called to in following Him, His promises to you, and that Heaven is your home. The Lord works through His Word, by the Holy Spirit in you, to transform you, fill you with joy, and guide you into all He created you for as His girl!

Isn't that amazing? Talk about a treasure! His Word – the Bible – is so, so, so important to knowing Jesus and living the life you were created for in Him! In the same way that a letter helps you know a friend better, a map helps you find a path, and food helps you grow strong – the Bible helps you know Jesus better, guides you into all He has called you to, strengthens you in Him, and so much more. Doesn't that make you want to dig into the Bible? As you look to His Word as your truth – instead of feelings, thoughts, culture, and lies of the enemy – this impacts your life in a powerful way! You are called to be a girl of the Word of God who is informed and transformed by truth. Let's dive in!

The Bible helps you know Jesus better, guides you into all He has called you to, strengthens you in Him, and so much more.

A Girl of the Word

A girl of the Word is what you want to be. Isn't it? You love Jesus and hang on His every word. Like Peter, you say to Jesus, *"...Lord, to whom shall we go? You have the words of eternal life."* (John 6:68) You know that the Bible is where you find the truth and show you are His disciple – *"...If you abide in my word, you are truly my dis-*

ciples…" (John 8:31) It is the Word of the One you love, belong to, and believe in. Your Jesus has spoken. You have the joy to open the Bible and listen to Him. You have the privilege, and opportunity, to base your life on it!

What It Is and Why It Is So Important

Okay, stop for a moment and ask, "Why is the Word of God so important?"

It is so key for you to see why His Word is so valuable – so you value it for the treasure it is! Otherwise, it is easy to turn to lesser things with your time and attention – and experience the loss of what you could receive from His Word. Just like you might not give much time or attention to drinking water unless you know the difference that it made to your life. You need it so much. Let's see why! Are you ready?

This is what you have in His Word:

- ⋙ It is God's Word.
- ⋙ God's Word is Truth. *"…Your word is truth."* (John 17:17)
- ⋙ It is God's Word to you.
- ⋙ You cannot know what is true on your own. It is only through listening to the One Who is Truth and speaks Truth in His Word – the Bible – that you can know Truth!
- ⋙ It shows you the Truth about Who your Jesus is, what He said, what He has done, who you are in Jesus, His promises, the life He has called you to as His, and more.
- ⋙ His Word is alive and brings life. *"For the word of God is living and active…"* (Hebrews 4:12)
- ⋙ His Word is unchanging. *"The grass withers, the flower*

fades, but the word of our God will stand forever."
(Isaiah 40:8)
≫ It is your lifeline – (John 6:68), foundation for your life
– (Matthew 7:24-27), guide – (Psalm 119:105), food for
your soul – (Matthew 4:4), and so much more!
≫ And so many more reasons!

Do you see a little glimpse of how important it is to consistently
fill your mind, heart, and life with the truth from God's Word? It is
very important!

Listen to this – what you believe and hold as truth massively
impacts your mind, your heart, your soul, how you live your life, and
your eternal destiny. So, make sure you know the Truth from Jesus,
from His Word!

Just like you need to eat breakfast every morning, you need
to faithfully prioritize time in the Bible –
because you see its importance in your
life with Jesus. Try turning to it before
you pick up your phone, look at social
media, read a book, etc. You will begin
to realize that it is your spiritual food and
hunger to fill your heart with the Word
above anything else! Jesus said, "...Man
shall not live by bread alone, but by every word that comes from the mouth of
God." (Matthew 4:4)

Knowing Truth in your head is good, but when it goes from your head to your heart, real life change happens.

When you open up your Bible and
read, the Holy Spirit works in your heart,
feeds your soul, and changes you! Thrilling, isn't it? And there are
life-transforming results when you do! One of my favorite results is
that the more you read the Bible, the more you will grow to love the
One Who it is about – the Lord Jesus.

I hope that by the time you finish this book, from all of the glimpses of His Word in here, you will be so in love with the Bible. And that, as a result, you will cling to it as your source of all the Truth your soul needs – because it points you to Jesus and fills your heart and mind with more of Him! *"Your word is a lamp to my feet and a light to my path."* (Psalm 119:105)

The Transformation in Your Life

Friend, grasp this: When you listen to Jesus in His Word, your heart and life are transformed by the Holy Spirit working within you. We looked before at the beautiful reality that the Bible is where you find truth and show you are His disciple: *"...If you abide in my word, you are truly my disciples..."* The verse continues and explains what the result will be: *"...And you will know the truth, and the truth will set you free."* (John 8:31-32)

So, picture this in your life: You want to know and be transformed by the Truth of the Word for yourself. You grab your Bible, open it, and begin to read. You come to know the Truth by reading. The Holy Spirit transforms your heart as you read – helping you to understand what you are reading, giving you spiritual power to receive it in faith, and applying it to you personally so that it goes from your head to your heart. As you go about your day, you experience the results of your changed heart flowing out in how you live. Isn't that incredible?

You see, knowing it in your head is good, but when it goes 12 inches down – from your head to your heart – is when real life change happens. Just like a seed when it is sown takes root, grows, and bears fruit, something that you personally know and believe grows and bears fruit in your life!

You will personally experience a life-long process of being transformed by the Word as you depend on Jesus and His Word being applied to your mind and heart by the Holy Spirit. Jesus has this for you! *"...Be transformed by the renewal of your mind..."* (Romans 12:2)

And, you know what? The more you are transformed, the more freeing it is! The more you are transformed, the more you will see like Jesus sees, love what He loves, think like He thinks, live like He lived, etc.! It is like a person seeing life through a new lens – but instead, you are seeing and living through a transformed mind and a changed heart. As a result, you grow in becoming more of who He created and called you to be in Him – a girl of the Word who is transformed by Truth! This is so beautiful, isn't it?

You Live What You Really Believe

It is powerful to realize that – you live what you really believe. Let's emphasize that again. You live what you really believe. Again, like we looked at before, that is why what you believe is so crucial, because it shapes how you live. That is why you want to know the truth about God, yourself, life, and eternity!

Let's look at some specific illustrations of how what you believe impacts what you do:

If you believe _____, then you will _____. So, for example:

>> If you believe that the Lord is in control, then you will not fear the future. *"My times are in your hand..."* (Psalm 31:15)

>> If you believe that Heaven is your home, *"...our citizenship is in heaven..."* (Philippians 3:20), then you will not invest all of your treasure here on earth.

When you live in what you believe, you experience the results of walking in faith in that area!

Now you try filling in a couple:

> "If I believe that _____, then I
> will _____
> _____."
>
> "If I believe that _____, then I
> will _____
> _____."

It can be so powerful in your life! Do you see how this could be life-changing? It is when you really know, believe, and live in the reality of God's Word that it will change how you live. You see, if my friend tells me I am welcome to eat the chocolate in the dish on her table, I could say that I believe my friend, but I prove I believe her when I actually eat a piece of that chocolate. Right? I then enjoy the results of the sweet flavor in my mouth. In the same way, you do this when you take Jesus at His Word, walk in faith, and experience the magnificent results!

Doesn't it make you want to run and hug your Bible?

Ways to Know and Live in His Truth

"…Be transformed by the renewal of your mind…" (Romans 12:2)

Okay, so you know and are transformed by Truth through the Word of God – the Bible – as the Holy Spirit works in you. Like I mentioned in an earlier chapter, if you do not have your own Bible, I encourage you to get one. You can read it for free online until you get one. It is so powerful when you are in it and have it in you!

Are you ready? Let's explore some powerful ways to know His

Truth! Just like a shovel helps you dig for gold, these are like tools that help you get to the treasure and results you long for!

Pray before you read the Word for the Lord to open your eyes of understanding. *"Open my eyes, that I may behold wondrous things out of your law (His Word)."* (Psalm 119:18) It is only by the Lord opening your eyes to His truth that your life is transformed. As you open your Bible to read, you can ask Jesus to open your mind and heart to understand what you are reading and for Him to do a work in your heart.

Read His Word. Read the Bible knowing the reality that it is the Word of the One you love – Jesus – and your source of Truth. Watch for Jesus to meet you in the pages! Read seeking to truly know Jesus, His Truth, and what He has for you. It is such a treasure to be able to read His Word for yourself!

When you read your Bible, it can be so helpful to ask these questions:

>> What did I read?
>> What does it tell me about Jesus and Who He is?
>> How does it transform me?
>> How can I live in it today?

You can record the answers in a journal if you want to! It can help you think it through and remember it better when you write it out. Reading your Bible is so powerful and important! It is life-changing! I encourage you to try to read your Bible daily.

Study His Word. When you study the Bible, you are taking time to look more closely at the Bible than when you are reading it. You are trying to dig deeper, to understand more fully what the Lord is saying. You can do this with a passage you really love, one you want to understand better, or one you have questions about. You can dig into the text by using study tools. Some helpful tools include a Bible dictionary to look up the meaning of words, cross-references to look up related verses, and Bible commentaries to explain the verses.

You could also do a Bible study with others. Getting into the Word with others is so powerful. Each person could share what the Lord is showing them. And it keeps you accountable to do it! *"All Scripture is breathed out by God and profitable for teaching, for re-proof, for correction, and for training in righteousness, that the man of God may be complete, equipped for every good work."* (2 Timo-thy 3:16-17)

Memorize His Word. It is so powerful to memorize God's Word and have it in your mind and heart. Think about how valu-able it has been when you have needed to memorize something so you remember it – your phone number, your birth date, etc. When you commit God's Word to your memory, it is putting the most im-portant information in your mind and heart. Then, it is there all of the time for you to think about, reference, be transformed by, and live from! You can memorize by reading it over and over, placing it somewhere you see it often, saying it out loud, or whatever way works for you! Try memorizing one Bible verse and see what a bless-ing it is! *"I have stored up your word in my heart, that I might not sin against you."* (Psalm 119:11)

Think about His Word. If you have memorized verses from the Bible, it is so powerful because you are able to think about it and ap-ply a verse wherever you are! You can be somewhere where you do not have your Bible, or be lying in bed in the dark, and still be able to think about His Word! Isn't that exciting?

Just yesterday I was sitting outside, and I did not have my Bible with me, but I was able to think about part of a verse that I love and was blessed by it because it was hidden in my heart! *"Let the word of Christ dwell in you richly…"* (Colossians 3:16) It can be so easy for our minds to go a million places, and some thoughts are not very helpful or can even be harmful. Think about His Word in your devotions, as you go through your day, and when you lie in bed at night – and allow Him to show you amazing things!

Pray His Word, ask Him to transform your heart with it, and ask Him for help to walk in, and apply it to, your life. You can ask the Holy Spirit to use what you just read in the Bible to transform your heart and give you the help to live in the reality of it! Another powerful thing is to actually pray the verse that He used to bless you that day. For example, if you read, *"Trust in the Lord with all your heart…"* (Proverbs 3:5), you could pray, "Dear Lord, please help me to trust in You with all of my heart…!" Do you see how that works? Your heart will be transformed when the power of His Word does a work in it! It is so important that His Word, and what it shows you, goes from your head to your heart – and then it will flow out in your life!

Seek to take one step to apply His Word with His help that day. James 1:22 says, *"…be doers of the word, and not hearers only…"* After you read your Bible, ask or pray, "What is one step I can take to apply it today?" and ask Jesus for His help to do that. Then take that step to apply it, and see what the Lord does!

Experience the transformation of His Word in your own life personally. As you respond to what He shows you from His Word, He will bring amazing transformation in your heart and life! You will be so blessed as you personally experience it!

This is so beautiful!

You need your Bible daily! Turn to it every day and in moments throughout the day. When you have a question or struggle, let it be the first place you turn. Run first to the Bible, not any other book, or anywhere else for answers. Read it, saying, "I believe You Jesus!" and then step out in faith, depending on His grace – and watch what He will do!

A Powerful Application Process to Try

So, let's walk through a process of reading and applying His Word together:

- ⫸ Grab your Bible.
- ⫸ Stop and ask the Lord to open your eyes to His Truth, apply it to your heart, and transform you.
- ⫸ Open to Psalm 63 and read verses 1-6.
- ⫸ As you read verse 3, you can respond to the Lord and say, "Your steadfast love is better than life, Jesus, and I praise you for it! Please help me to live in the reality of that love today and love You in return!"
- ⫸ As you walk through the day, seek to remember that truth about His love and live in it. You can write the verse on a card and carry it with you during the day!
- ⫸ Watch what the Holy Spirit does!

I am so looking forward to what the Lord has in store as you do this!

Ask for His help to live in what He shows you by His grace. Depend on Him for the power of His life within you, and take a step to live in it! See what He does. Can you feel the anticipation rising?

Choose to listen to — and believe — Jesus above all of the other voices in your life!

Just Go For It

The most powerful thing is to actually do it – pick up your Bible, pray for Jesus to meet you, and read. Go for it right now! That is the key. While spending lots of time in the Bible is amazing, even a couple of minutes will do such wonders!

(You are so welcome – and encouraged – to put this book down and pick up your Bible!)

Listen to Jesus

It is so important that you are listening to Jesus! Choose to listen to – and believe – Jesus above all of the other voices in your life! It is like when you tune into a specific radio station. There are many stations you can choose to listen to, right? In life, you want to listen to Jesus! Be very careful what voices you are listening to. You see, your life is profoundly impacted by who you are listening to because it impacts your mind, heart, and life.

When you listen to Jesus, it is wonderful – it results in freedom, joy, and peace! When you listen to your feelings, thoughts, lies of the devil, culture, etc., you will experience confusion, instability, and bondage. Stop and think. Who are you listening to? Listen to Jesus! Listen to Jesus in His Word – the Bible. Believe Jesus above all of the other voices. Ask, "What do You say, Jesus?" and then believe Him above other voices! Respond to Him, "Jesus, I believe You above anything else." Make, "I believe You, Jesus!" a motto. *"...This is my beloved Son; listen to him."* (Mark 9:7)

Faith in His Word — Believing and Owning His Word for Yourself

Oh, faith is so important. But what exactly is faith? Faith is essentially believing and trusting, or depending on, what God has said in His Word. So, this can look like reading the Word and believing it in your heart, saying, "Jesus, I believe You!" Faith is evidenced by depending on His Word and going and walking in it in daily life. Isn't that so powerful?

Friend, you exercise faith when you personally look into the Bible, and then own and believe His Word for yourself – not just because someone told you about it! Do you see how powerful this is?

Faith is personally knowing what you believe and why, so you can say, "I believe this because my God said it. I have read it in His

Word and know it is Truth. It is not just because someone told me – but because I have experienced it. It is my Truth now. I believe it, and it has changed my life! I will stand on it, no matter what." Then, no matter where you are or what you face, you can cling by faith to what you know is Truth! You want to personally know it, believe it, own it, walk in it, and experience it. When you do this, amazing results will come in your life!

Pause for a moment and reflect on your own personal beliefs. You can ask yourself:

≫ "Who – or what – am I truly believing?"

≫ "What am I basing my belief on?"

≫ "What does how I am living show about what I truly believe?"

≫ "What is the fruit in my life?"

It is so powerful when you exercise faith in Jesus and His Word, and see what results He brings in your life. Let His Word be yours by faith!

What Can Hold You Back from Reading the Word

Many things can hold you back from reading and living in the Word of God! It is like roadblocks standing in the way of you making discoveries that will impact your life. Realize these are things holding you back from something that will change and bless your life!

Things that are obstacles include: not seeing the value of the Word, not knowing how to read it, believing other things instead of it, getting distracted with other things, forgetting to read it, choosing wrong priorities in your heart, and use of time – and more!

What is holding you back? You can write it here:

_____

_____

_____

Ask Jesus for His help to move beyond that and go read His Word in faith! You will experience the value as you do!

Struggles You May Face with False Truths

Okay, are you ready for some powerful stuff?

You want to be a girl of the Word, who believes Jesus above anything else – more than feelings, thoughts, what people say, lies of the enemy, etc.! You have a million messages thrown at you every day, like popcorn flying from a popcorn popper, saying, "Believe me!" Those messages are often changing, untrue, and not from Jesus. The Bible is the one place you can go and know that it is always true. Isn't that a comfort?

We are going to look at Truth vs. "false truths" (also known as lies)! Sources of false truths that you can face include:

- ≫ lies of your enemy the devil – "*...The devil... when he lies, he speaks out of his own character, for he is a liar and the father of lies.*" (John 8:44)
- ≫ feelings – "*...For whenever our heart condemns us, God is greater than our heart, and he knows everything.*" (1 John 3:20)
- ≫ thoughts – "*Trust in the LORD with all your heart, and do not lean on your own understanding.*" (Proverbs 3:5)
- ≫ culture's messages that are opposite to God's Word – "*We destroy arguments and every lofty opinion raised*

against the knowledge of God, and take every thought captive to obey Christ..." (2 Corinthians 10:5)

≫ people speaking false things – *"...The Lord – knows the thoughts of man, that they are but a breath."* (Psalm 94:11)

≫ and other things!

What is a "false truth" (lie) that you are struggling with right now?

_____

_____

_____

It is like a bunch of people dressed up like someone trying to make you believe they are the real person, and they are not! If you know the real person, you can spot the fake ones, right? Your enemy – the devil – does not want you to know the Truth, because if you know it, believe it, and live in it by the power of the Holy Spirit, your life and the world around you will never be the same! His goal is to deceive you to make you believe his lies. I know that I personally have listened to and believed the lies of the enemy, thoughts I have in my mind, and my feelings. The results of believing them have been discouragement, bondage, fear, etc. Then, when the Lord has brought me Truth from His Word in the place of those things, He has brought me freedom, joy, worship, power, and strength. I have been so grateful for the times He has used His Word to free me from the devil's lies! It is so powerful.

It is so important for you to be able to identify and embrace truth instead of "false truths" (lies)!

Truth vs. Lies Test

Are you ready to have some fun?

Below is a list of thoughts that I would love for you to read and then to respond to and say if they are truth or lies. If it is true, you can circle the "T" by the statement, and if it is a lie, you can circle the "L" by the statement. Then I would love to have you write a Bible verse on the line provided that supports a true statement or with a Bible verse that counteracts a false statement with Truth.

When you are finished, there is an answer key at the end of the chapter!

"No one loves me." T/L

_____

_____

_____

_____

"God has an incredible plan for my life." T/L

_____

_____

_____

"God could not forgive me." T/L

_____

_____

_____

"I can find total fulfillment in Christ." T/L

_____

_____

"I need to earn God's love." T/L

_____

_____

"The Lord rewards those who diligently seek Him." T/L

_____

_____

"I am all alone." T/L

_____

_____

This approach of evaluating thoughts or statements will help keep you grounded in Truth.

Have you ever felt a dollar bill before? When people are training to work at a bank, they are given real money to feel over and over until they know it so well. Then the trainers slip in a fake piece of money and the ones being trained are able to feel that it is not a genuine dollar bill because they are so well trained in what real money feels like. The more you know the Truth of God's Word, the more easily you will be able to identify the lies of the enemy and false truths when they come to you!

While it can be easy to turn to other things as truth, they will always deceive you and bear bad fruit in your life. Again, you can turn to Jesus and say like Peter said to Jesus, *"...You have the words of eternal life."* (John 6:68), and you will find the Truth that sets you free!

You want to be a girl of the Word who believes Jesus above anything else — and is beautifully transformed by His Truth!

Look at these people the Bible talks about – *"...they received the word with all eagerness, examining the Scriptures daily to see if these things were so."* (Acts 17:11) That is how you want to be! Take everything back to the Word of God to see if it is true. (Including everything that you read in this book!) It must line up with the Word of God. The Bible is the standard of Truth – and your standard of Truth as His girl!

The Impact on Your Life When You Believe False Truths

Do you know that when you do believe false truths, there are difficult results in your life? Just like when you believe Truth and there are favorable results in your life. For example, if you believe your feelings – one day you might feel like Jesus is not with you, and one day you might feel like He is. But His Word tells you, *"...I will never leave you nor forsake you."* (Hebrews 13:5) Or, if you believe it when you feel like or think that God does not love you, it will change how you relate to Him and you will live scared. But, if you believe Him when He says, *"I have loved you with an everlasting love…"* (Jeremiah 31:3), you will relate to Him freely and live secure in His love.

The Bible tells you what you can do when lies come into your mind. *"We destroy arguments and every lofty opinion raised against the knowledge of God, and take every thought captive to obey Christ…"* (2 Corinthians 10:5) When lies come into your mind, you can choose to respond by saying, "I believe Jesus over this thought, feeling, lie, etc.!" Beautiful results will come against those false truths. Jesus brings transformation from lies to Truth through His Word the Bible. *"Do not be conformed to this world, but be transformed by the renewal of your mind…"* (Romans 12:2) You want to be a girl of the Word who believes Jesus above anything else – more than feelings, thoughts, what people say, lies of the enemy, etc. – and is beautifully transformed by His Truth!

Picture It in Your Life

How would it change your everyday life if you were a girl of the Word? Picture as you walk through your day, feel different things, read different things online, hear the words to different songs, etc., how the Bible can be like a filter that you run things through to know if they are true or not!

Here is an example of how this can look in real life:

You wake up feeling down and battling doubts about whether or not the Lord loves you. At this point you have a choice. You can listen to your feelings and doubts, and let the enemy, culture, and other voices bring you deeper into that struggle by being *"…conformed to the world…"* (Romans 12:2). Or, you can listen to Jesus and His Word and be *"…transformed by the renewing of your mind…"* (Romans 12:2). How? You can open your Bible and find a verse like Jeremiah 31:3, *"…I have loved you with an everlasting love…"* You can read the verse, fix your mind on its Truth, ask the

Lord to apply it to your heart, choose to believe it, walk in the reality of it, and experience the peace and joy of being assured of the Lord's love!

Do you see how amazing this is and how this works?

A Sweet Thing

I love that the more you know the Bible and have it in your head and heart, the more the Holy Spirit can bring it to mind when you need it! For example, one time I was sitting on the floor in my bedroom and thinking about what my future would hold, and the Holy Spirit brought Jeremiah 29:11 to mind: *"For I know the plans I have for you, declares the LORD, plans to prosper you, and not to harm you, to give you a future and a hope."* It was just what I needed at that moment and it brought so much comfort!

Jesus and His Word are amazing! You need Him and His Word so much!

You Want to Be a Girl of the Word

Here's the thing, friend — you want to live a life that is transformed by His Truth, solid in His Word, and walking in the realities He has told you there.

You want to be a girl of the Word who:

>> bases her life on Jesus and what He has said in His Word.

>> refuses to be led by her emotions, accept her thoughts as the final authority, trust experience to be a measuring line, believe what culture holds out as the truth, or buy into the enemy's lies.

>> takes her God at His Word and lives with Spirit-empowered faith.

⇒ experiences the vibrant life she was made for as she follows the One Who is life and speaks the words of life – Jesus.

I'm in. Are you? Let's listen to Jesus again, *"...If you abide in my word, you are truly my disciples, and you will know the truth, and the truth will set you free."* (John 8:31-32)

Review of the Truth

This is so important and powerful. Do you see the transformation that comes in your life the more you know, believe, and live in God's Word? When you build your life on Jesus and His Word, you will be secure. If you build your life on the lies of the enemy, your feelings, etc., you will be unstable and led into struggles.

In the Bible, Jesus shares these powerful words:

> *"Everyone then who hears these words of mine and does them will be like a wise man who built his house on the rock. And the rain fell, and the floods came, and the winds blew and beat on that house, but it did not fall, because it had been founded on the rock. And everyone who hears these words of mine and does not do them will be like a foolish man who built his house on the sand. And the rain fell, and the floods came, and the winds blew and beat against that house, and it fell, and great was the fall of it."* (Matthew 7:24-27)

Build your life on Jesus and His Word – the Bible – and live it out! You need His Truth all of the time and in every area of your life. This is your call as His girl to be in His Word, have it in you, and allow it to transform your heart and life by the Holy Spirit!

Application Step

Take a Truth from a Bible verse that you need to place in your heart. Write it on a piece of paper – a card, sticky note, etc. – and place it somewhere you will see it often. Then you can also memorize it, think about it, and pray it to the Lord! Watch the difference it makes in your life!

A Call to Action

This is so important as you walk as His girl – to know, believe and walk in His Truth. His Word applied to your heart by the Spirit is the way to know Him, the Truth by which to be transformed, and the guide to this life that He has called you to in Him. Ask for the Spirit's help to read, believe, and be transformed by it, and to walk in it daily.

Go open your Bible! This is so life-changing!

Will you personally look to Jesus in His Word, ask Him to transform your life with His Truth, and watch Him work? As you do, you will be transformed by Truth as Christ's girl who is a girl of the Word!

TRUTH VS. LIES ANSWER KEY

- "No one loves me." – LIE – "...I have loved you with everlasting love..." (Jeremiah 31:3)
- "God has an incredible plan for my life." – TRUE – "For I know the plans I have for you, declares the LORD, plans for welfare and not for evil, to give you a future and a hope." (Jeremiah 29:11)
- "God could not forgive me." – LIE – "If we confess our sins, he is faithful and just to forgive us our sins and to cleanse us from all unrighteousness." (1 John 1:9)
- "I can find total fulfillment in Christ." – TRUE – "...He satisfies the longing soul..." (Psalm 107:9)
- "I need to earn God's love." – LIE – "...God shows his love for us in that while we were still sinners, Christ died for us." (Romans 5:8)
- "The Lord rewards those who seek Him." – TRUE – "...He rewards those who seek him." (Hebrews 11:6)
- "I am all alone." – LIE – "...I will never leave you..." (Hebrews 13:5)

STUDY GUIDE

What was one thing that was especially helpful to you in this chapter?

_____

_____

_____

What is one step that you will take today to apply it to your own life?

_____

_____

What is one struggle that you face in this area that you can ask Jesus to help you overcome?

_____

_____

Look up these Bible verses and write what Jesus shows you:

•   John 8:31-32

_____

_____

_____

•   John 17:17

_____

_____

- Isaiah 40:8

_____

_____

_____

Pray or write out a prayer of response to Jesus.

_____

_____

_____

_____

Write the Focus Statement for this chapter.

_____

_____

_____

_____

You can write any additional thoughts here.

_____

_____

_____

_____

THE MORE YOU GROW

*the more
Jesus
will show*

CHAPTER 6

Growing in Jesus

THE PROCESS OF BECOMING LIKE AND RADIATING JESUS FROM THE INSIDE OUT

"...He who began a good work in you will bring it to completion at the day of Jesus Christ." (Philippians 1:6)

....

Who are you growing to be like?

Just like a baby is always a human, when you become Christ's, that is secure – you are always His. Growth in Him comes from that place. Growth does not make you His, but is proof you are His. Like a baby matures and begins to walk, talk, etc., so Jesus matures you in your walk with Him!

As Christ's girl, you have this beautiful reality:

When you come to Jesus in salvation and become His girl, He begins a beautiful lifelong work in your heart to grow you to become more and more like Him – causing you to thrive more in the vibrant life

109

He created you for in Him, shine His beauty from the inside out, and glorify Him in your life. Jesus is growing you, working in your heart, bringing transformation — and blossoming you to increasingly thrive in what you were created for in Him as His girl!

Incredible, isn't it? You have this precious promise, "...he who began a good work in you will bring it to completion at the day of Jesus Christ." (Philippians 1:6) What an amazing thing! Jesus makes you His, and then He grows you for the rest of your life here on earth in a transforming way. Jesus is forming you into a girl becoming more and more like Him, a girl who is thriving more and more in Jesus as He works in you, a girl who is growing in experiencing His joy, shining His beauty, living in His freedom, and so much more. This is a transformation with beautiful results! Isn't this exciting?

Jesus makes you His, and then He grows you for the rest of your life here on earth in a transforming way.

Let's make sure this is so clear from the beginning — Jesus loved you before you ever trusted Him — even when you were still a sinner. "...God shows his love for us in that while we were still sinners, Christ died for us." (Romans 5:8) He loves you as His girl, and you cannot earn or lose His love. Because He loves you, He wants you to grow and to experience more and more of the life He created you for in Him. Does that make sense?

And this is exciting — Him working in you is proof that you are His. True spiritual growth is proof that you are His, and His Holy Spirit is within you. You see the fruit in your life that you are His — like a branch of an apple tree that is growing and bearing apples is proof it belongs to the apple tree. Growth and works do not make you His – His work in you, the growth He brings in your life, and the fruit from your life are proof that you are His. So, when you see His work in you, you can rejoice!

It is an incredible thing that the Lord of the universe is working in you to grow you in Him! He has so much in store for you. Doesn't this make you grateful for the growth and give you a desire to embrace it?

A Call to Transformation

Jesus is doing a transforming work in you to make you more like Himself! Here is the extraordinary thing – He wants to transform you. He wants to make you into all that He has called you to be in Him! You want to become like Jesus and be shaped into all He has for you, right? *"And we all, with unveiled face, beholding the glory of the Lord, are being transformed into the same image from one degree of glory to another. For this comes from the Lord who is the Spirit."* (2 Corinthians 3:18)

Jesus Cares About Your Heart

Friend, listen to this: Jesus cares about your heart. It is so important to understand that Jesus cares the most about the condition of your heart and your relationship with Him. The rest of your life will flow out of your heart. Let's say that again. The state of your heart and your relationship with Jesus impacts all of the rest of your life. Proverbs 4:23 tells you, *"Keep your heart with all vigilance, for from it flow the springs of life."*

Jesus is not calling you to just modify your behavior. He wants to transform you from the heart – from the inside out! He does not just want you to reform (clean up your act) or to conform (following rules on the outside), but to be transformed by Him in your heart in a way that flows out in your life. When your heart is transformed by

Jesus in you, it will result in transformed living, making you like Him in how you live. It is like a child who does things from their heart with joy because they love and trust their parents, instead of simply behaving well on the outside to avoid discipline but not being happy about it on the inside.

So, for example, He wants to work in your heart to transform you, so you love His Kingdom! Then it will be a much more natural outflow in your life to share Him with others. He wants your heart and to bring growth in your heart – and for your living will be an outflow of that! Ask the Lord for a soft and moldable heart that is sensitive to the Holy Spirit and allows Jesus to work in you.

You Cannot Do This on Your Own

Okay, are you ready for something that is so key for you to understand? You cannot be transformed in your heart – or produce fruit in your life – on your own strength. Striving with your own strength to change yourself is like demanding a water bottle to produce and pour out water on its own. That is silly, exhausting, and impossible, right? It takes a work of His Spirit in your heart and life. This keeps you dependent on Jesus and is so sweet! You are empowered, and He is glorified. He does amazing things!

In John 15, Jesus gives you a beautiful picture of how this works when He says, *"I am the true vine, and my Father is the vinedresser... Abide in me, and I in you. As the branch cannot bear fruit by itself, unless it abides in the vine, neither can you, unless you abide in me. I am the vine; you are the branches. Whoever abides in me and I in him, he it is that bears much fruit, for apart from me you can do nothing."* (John 15:1, 4-5) Jesus is the Vine, you are the branch. As you abide (to remain) in Him, He works, and brings beautiful fruit in your life! Apart from Him, you cannot produce fruit.

Just like the verse we looked at earlier says, *"We...are being transformed... For this comes from the Lord who is the Spirit."* (2 Corinthians 3:18) And listen to this verse, too: *"...for it is God who works in you, both to will and to work for his good pleasure."* (Philippians 2:13)

Only Jesus can work this transformation in you by His Spirit. In response to His life working in you, you embrace Him and His work in your life. You pursue and cooperate with His transforming work. Ask Him, "Jesus, I need You to work in me. Please grow me and help me to pursue you." Have you ever tried to curl your hair with a curling iron not plugged in? There were no results, right? But, when you have it plugged in and the power is running

Only Jesus can work this transformation in you by His Spirit.

through it, it brings beautiful results. As you depend on Jesus to work in you and join Him by His power, He will do beautiful things! *"Now may the God of peace himself sanctify you completely... He who calls you is faithful; he will surely do it."* (1 Thessalonians 5:23-24)

The Role of the Holy Spirit

It is so important for you to understand the role of the Holy Spirit in your life as His girl. The Trinity is the Father, the Son, and the Holy Spirit – God the Father (Father), God the Son (Jesus), and God the Spirit (Holy Spirit). All three are one God, and they are equal in importance – and they each have and play unique roles in your spiritual life. *"The grace of the Lord Jesus Christ and the love of God and the fellowship of the Holy Spirit be with you all."* (2 Corinthians 13:14) You receive the Holy Spirit when you become His girl. The Holy Spirit is the life of God within you, guiding you in Truth (the Bible), transforming your heart, empowering you to live for Him, and more! As you listen to, respond to, and follow Him, He does amazing things in your heart, growth, and life! *"...Not by might, nor by power, but by my Spirit, says the Lord of hosts."* (Zechariah 4:16)

The Fruit in Your Life

Just like sowing seeds in your garden takes time for a plant to grow and produce fruit, it takes time to grow in your Christian walk. Like we looked at before, you become more like Him, as your heart continues to be transformed. His life then flows out from your life, and He is glorified!

This is a peek at the fruit that comes in your life as He transforms you:

You become more like Jesus. After you have spent time with a friend, have you ever had someone say, "I can tell you were just with that friend because you are talking just like her!"? I want people to say, "I can tell you spent time with Jesus because you are so much like Him!" It is the beauty of Jesus' life, in and shining from, you! (We will look more at true beauty below). This happens more and more as you grow in likeness to Jesus! I want this, don't you?

You see and experience the fruit of the Spirit in your life. *"...The fruit of the Spirit is love, joy, peace, patience, kindness, goodness, faithfulness, gentleness, self-control..."* (Galatians 5:22-23)

Your living matches your identity more and more. It is a joy, and there is so much freedom there! It is so transforming. It leads to living more and more like Jesus called you to as an outflow of His transforming work in your heart. (We will look more at this in the *Living as His Girl* chapter!)

In addition to these results of His transformation in you, growth in Jesus also:

>> builds you up in Jesus
>> deepens you in vibrancy, thriving, and life
>> strengthens and guards you against sin
>> helps to overcome sin
>> and more!

Isn't that amazing? I want that fruit in my life so much, don't you?

Just like people can often see the likeness of a parent in a child as it grows, I want people to see Jesus in me more and more as He grows me! Or, like people can tell who the artist is by their artwork, I want people to see Jesus and His handiwork in me! I want to grow in becoming like and glorifying Jesus all of my life, don't you? This is so amazing – Jesus wants to grow you so that you think like He thinks, love like He loves, and act like He acts! Isn't that encouraging? I hope so!

Thriving in Jesus More and More

Jesus wants to continue to work in you so that you'll thrive and live more and more fully in what He created you to be as His girl! He is helping you become more like Him, growing you in experiencing His joy, shining His beauty, living in His freedom, and so much more. This is transformation with beautiful results! *"...That your love may abound more and more, with knowledge and all discernment, so that you may approve what is excellent, and so be pure and blameless for the day of Christ, filled with the fruit of righteousness that comes through Jesus Christ, to the glory and praise of God."* (Philippians 1:9) The deeper you can grow and thrive, the better. You want to walk more fully in this and experience this in your life. Seek to embrace it!

True Beauty

True beauty is Jesus in your life. You want true beauty – and this is it! 1 Peter 3:3-4 says, *"Your adornment must not be merely external–braiding the hair, and wearing gold jewelry, or putting on dresses; but let it be the hidden person of the heart, with the imperishable quality of a gentle and quiet spirit, which is precious in the sight of God."* And Proverbs 31:30 reminds us, *"Charm is deceitful, and beauty is vain, but a woman who fears the LORD is to be praised."*

The beauty of Jesus in and through you only grows more beautiful with time as He shines in and from you more and more! It can be so easy in our culture to focus on the outside appearance and how you look, can't it? It is not that you should never brush your hair or seek to look nice, but it is realizing that the transformation of your heart, and Jesus shining from it, is the truest, most lasting beauty.

Imagine yourself as an elderly lady – when your youthful appearance has faded and you are getting closer to the end of your life. Quite the thought, isn't it? What will truly matter to you then? What truly matters now? What will truly matter in eternity? Who is Jesus calling you to be? Every step of growth in Jesus now will bear fruit for the rest of your life on earth – however long it is. Physical beauty will fade with time. But the beauty of Jesus will shine from you more and more over time as you grow in Him! There will be more of His light in your eyes, His love radiating through you, and His likeness in your actions.

Understanding this will compel you to invest more time in seeking inner beauty – spending time with Jesus, reading your Bible, etc. – than in seeking outer beauty – curling your hair, choosing an outfit, etc.. The beauty of Jesus in you is lasting beauty – the kind that is eternal! "...Christ in you, the hope of glory." (Colossians 1:27) This true beauty of Jesus in you results in His glory, your joy, and the blessing of others!

How to Embrace Growth

So, how do I embrace this work of Jesus in my life? Let's take a look!

Listen to this: While Jesus does the transforming work in you, He gives you the calling to pursue and embrace that growth by the power of His Spirit in you. You both have a role! He works in you to draw your heart towards growth. Empowered by His Spirit in you, you respond and seek growth as a result. Through that, He works to bring transformation. Do you see how that works?

*"And God is able to make all grace abound to you, so that hav-
ing all sufficiency in all things at all times, you may abound in
every good work."* (2 Corinthians 9:8)

"…God gave the growth." (1 Corinthians 3:6)

He has given you wonderful tools to embrace growth! Like with
a cup that brings you water, you make use of these tools as things
through which you receive more of Jesus and His work in you.
Through them, He meets you, works in you, and then bears fruit in
your life. They are a gift! Let's call them "Growth Tools."

As you saw in the chapter on your personal relationship with
Jesus, some very important growth tools include:

⟫ asking Him for His help and for Him to make Himself
real to you.
⟫ making Him your #1 priority.
⟫ spending personal time with Him.
⟫ reading the Bible – His Word to you.
⟫ talking with Jesus in prayer.
⟫ walking with Him through the day.
⟫ studying, memorizing, and thinking about Scripture.

Those are wonderful tools, aren't they? They are some of the
main and most important tools! You want to really embrace them –
and daily is the best! Feel free to go back and review them!

Now, we get the joy of looking at some other powerful tools
that Jesus works through to help you grow in Him! Get ready to see
these incredible tools. Here we go!

Ask Him to grow you. You ask Jesus to work in your heart and
grow you because you know it is Him doing the transforming work
in you by His Spirit. You cannot do it on your own! *"…Increase our
faith…"* (Luke 17:5) *"Create in me a clean heart, O God…"* (Psalm
51:10) It is His joy to answer! He will do amazing things. *"…God who*

gives the growth..." (1 Corinthians 3:7) You could ask Him, "Jesus, please work in me and grow me in You!"

Finding fellowship and community with others who are His. It is so important that you spend time with people who are seeking the Lord and who will help you in your walk with the Lord! This can be through your church and other ways. If you do not have regular contact with girls with the same heart of seeking Jesus, you might want to think about taking the step and starting a Bible or spiritual growth book study! This can give you encouragement in seeking the Lord as you have fellowship with other girls who are desiring to follow Him. (You could even start a spiritual growth book study with this book!) *"But exhort one another every day, as long as it is called 'today,' that none of you may be hardened by the deceitfulness of sin."* (Hebrews 3:13) (We will talk more about relationships and friendships in the *Living as His Girl* chapter.)

Set up accountability. I would strongly encourage you to find someone to hold you accountable for seeking and loving the Lord. It will help you stay on track more than you could ever imagine! So, it could look like this – decide on what to hold each other accountable for (spending time reading your Bible, memorizing Scripture, etc.) → plan a regular check-in time (weekly, every 2 weeks, every month) to connect and report how it is going → follow through → and keep doing it!

When Jesus was drawing my heart to go deeper in my relationship with Him, I met a girl who I could tell loved Jesus, too. We decided to hold each other accountable for memorizing and thinking about Bible verses. We called each other every other week to check up on each other, and we had such a sweet fellowship in Jesus. It was a powerful help in my growth in Jesus. It can be a powerful help for you, too!

Become part of a solid church and listen to Biblical preaching. Attend and become involved in a church where Jesus is glorified, the Bible is preached, and it is based on the clear, true Gospel.

This can be used powerfully by the Lord to grow you in knowing, loving, and becoming like Jesus. God designed the church as a place where you can hear the preaching of His Word, worship Him, be in fellowship with the family of God, and have the joy of serving! *"…Not neglecting to meet together, as is the habit of some, but encouraging one another, and all the more as you see the Day drawing near."* (Hebrews 10:25)

Worship Jesus. You can worship Jesus through singing and prayer. Worship is declaring the worth of someone or something! You can worship Him by singing worship songs to Him. You can also worship Him by praying, "Jesus, You are amazing! I worship You that You are _____." – and list a quality that you love about Him – that He is loving, faithful, etc.. Isn't this special? This is so powerful because it turns your mind and heart to Who Jesus is! *"Ascribe to the Lord the glory due his name; worship the Lord…"* (Psalm 29:2)

Remind yourself of the Gospel. The Gospel is the good news of Jesus dying in your place to pay the punishment for your sins and offering you grace and eternal life in Him. It is what saves you, and it is also what sustains you for every moment of your sanctification after that. You are His. Then that same Gospel – the Truth that you need Jesus and He is enough – is what empowers and informs you to live from it to know, grow in, and follow Jesus! It is so helpful to remind yourself of it every day. Reminding yourself of the Gospel truth – you can periodically think about what the Gospel represents for your life with God. You can try something like this:

> I was separated from God by my sin. Jesus died on the cross to pay the penalty for my sin. When I turned away from my sin and received Jesus' forgiveness, He saved me from eternal separation from Him, giving me a new life in Jesus, now and forever.

Seek growth with genuine faith. A faith that believes Jesus, what He says, and what He promises to do. *"And without faith it is impossible to please him, for whoever would draw near to God must believe that he exists and that he rewards those who seek him."* (Hebrews 11:6) He brings beautiful things!

Fill your soul with things that encourage your walk with and growth in Him. These include reading, listening to messages, worship music, etc., that encourage your heart in Jesus. Think of a seed. If you sow a seed for an orange tree, you will get an orange. If you sow a thistle seed, you will get a thistle, right? In the same way, if you sow seeds of things that feed your soul in Jesus, like we looked at above, there will be good fruit.

Imagine you had two puppies. Happy thought, isn't it? What if you fed one a lot of really quality food, but you fed the other one garbage and only a little good food. Which one would grow strong and vibrant? The one you fed a lot with really quality food, right? That is what it is like with your soul and walk with Jesus.

What you feed – your walk with Jesus or your sinful human nature – will grow the most. What are you feeding right now – your walk with Jesus or your sinful human nature? Feed your walk with Jesus! *"Do not be deceived: God is not mocked, for whatever one sows, that will he also reap. **For the one who sows to his own flesh will from the flesh reap corruption, but the one who sows to the Spirit will from the Spirit reap eternal life.** And let us not grow weary of doing good, for in due season we will reap, if we do not give up."* (Galatians 6:7-9, emphasis added)

Here is a brief list of additional helpful tools that we will get to look at in chapters to come:

≫ Have a spiritual mentor to disciple you in Jesus.
≫ Share Jesus with others and serve Jesus.
≫ Journal His work in your life.
≫ Choose friends who will encourage you in Jesus.

This list is just the beginning! Are there "Growth Tools" that help you grow in Him? You can list them here:

_____

_____

_____

We could talk about each of these wonderful tools for a while – and there are many other helpful tools. I encourage you to look more into how you can embrace them in a way that will draw you closer to Jesus! You will have a lifetime to go deeper into them – as the Spirit works through them to grow you in Him. You could also ask people you know who are following Jesus what has been helpful to them!

As you embrace them, keep in mind the goal – to know, grow in, become like, and follow your Jesus. This is the goal! The more you make use of these tools, the more you will see the results and desire to do them!

The Lord has used – and continues to use – these tools to transform my life and grow me in Him! Countless times I have opened my Bible, talked with Him in prayer, spent time alone with Him, and He has met me, given me more of Himself, transformed my heart, and changed me. I will need them until the day that I die – because I will need Jesus for that long, and for eternity! I have seen Him do the same for many girls. He can do the same for you!

Do It

It is good to talk about these growth tools, but it is only when you do them yourself that they make an impact on your life. It's like brushing your teeth. You can't just talk about brushing. You must brush them to get clean teeth. It is important that we don't just talk about them. We must do them! Every bit makes a difference. Even grabbing two minutes in the Word makes a difference! Remember, growing takes time. Go do it!

And it is important to use the tools even when you do not feel like doing them. I know we want to desire to do them, but sometimes you just need to do them because they are good for you. If you do not feel like doing it, still do it. Just like a runner preparing for a race needs to run, whether they feel like it or not — knowing the results they want! When you do use the growth tools, you will see the fruit of your faithfulness, and you will find it increases your desire to do them.

Picture It in Your Life

I want you to pause for a second and think of one of the growth tools. Picture how you will apply it to your life and the difference it could make. Think of one step you will take. Take that step. See what Jesus does!

So, for example, you could think of the power of accountability. Picture how helpful it would be to have a friend who would check in on you to see if you have been reading the Bible. This accountability friend would help encourage you to get into the Word. Think of how you would be transformed. Now, think of the step of calling a friend and asking her to hold you accountable for reading your Bible every day. Call that friend and ask her! Do you see how it works?

You want to receive the Lord's grace to help you take action to actually apply one of these tools and experience the results!

Which one are you going to choose?

_____

_____

_____

What step are you going to take to apply it?

_____

_____

Write "Did it!" on this line when you have done it.

_____

A Tool — The Power Question

When considering if a choice is going to be helpful or hurtful in your walk with Jesus, this question is so powerful to ask:

> "Will this help me grow in Jesus — or will it draw me away from Him?"

Maybe you are wondering if you should listen to a certain song, watch a certain movie, etc. Asking this question will be so helpful! The answer to the question will help you determine what you should do.

What is a situation you could use this power question on right now?

_____

_____

_____

"So flee youthful passions and pursue righteousness, faith, love, and peace, along with those who call on the Lord from a pure heart." (2 Timothy 2:22)

This question can be so helpful to use as you seek to grow in Jesus!

Fruit Comes Over Time

Because you need Jesus daily, it is so powerful to seek growth and to use the gift of these tools daily. Just like you need to take time to care for your body every day to grow strong and stay healthy – by eating, sleeping, etc. – even more importantly, you need to care for your soul! Daily health steps and patterns add up and bear fruit, right? Even if you cannot remember what you had for breakfast yesterday, you know it nourished you. It is the same with the beautiful transformation the Lord pours into you through these growth tools into your life. The more you do them, the more you will see the fruit and desire to do them more!

All good things take investment and effort. Think of a relationship you want to deepen, muscles you want to strengthen, etc. – you have to invest in them. You cannot just sit around by yourself on the couch and hope it happens, right? You need to take the energy you have and go for it! Fruit will come.

What Holds You Back from Growth in Jesus

As you walk this walk with Jesus and this journey of growth in Him, there will be things that seek to hinder your growth.

The things that can hold you back can include:

>> distraction with less important things (sleep, projects, entertainment, social media, spending time online)
>> lack of desire for it
>> trying to do it in your own strength
>> not knowing how to do it
>> not knowing or believing the importance of it

⫸ doubting the difference it will make

⫸ guilt over not doing it in the past

⫸ and more!

So, for example, this can be believing that reading another chapter of a book you are reading will bring you more joy than spending time with Jesus. So, you skip your time with Him. This comes from forgetting your goal of seeking for a deeper joy in Jesus that nothing else can give you! Or, it can be getting distracted by projects

He welcomes you with open arms and is delighted to have you seek Him in this very moment!

or things happening in your life. Or anything else that you face in your life that holds you back from Jesus.

We all face these obstacles. It is helpful to recognize them so we can address them!

What are the things that are holding you back right now?

_____

_____

_____

Bring these to Jesus and ask Him for His help! You cannot fight them with your own strength, but He can give you the grace to overcome them and walk more and more in the freedom He purchased for you on the cross! *"...Not by might, nor by power, but by my Spirit, says the LORD of hosts."* (Zechariah 4:6) We all face these things in some way or another. Usually, the more important that something is to your spiritual growth, the greater the enemy will want to hold you back and distract you. Receive Jesus' help to push past it and watch His beautiful work!

125

Friend, listen closely to this — if you have not been spending time on these tools pursuing Jesus and growth in Him — ever, or have not for a while — know that He is not standing there with His arms crossed. Rather, He welcomes you with open arms and is delighted to have you seek Him today, and in this very moment! Know that Jesus is by your side all of the way in this growth process and delights in helping you take the next step with Him! *"For I, the LORD your God, hold your right hand; it is I who say to you, 'Fear not, I am the one who helps you.'"* (Isaiah 41:13) Isn't that such a joy and comfort?

On Facing Sin in Your Life

Now, let's take a moment to focus on something important in your life as His girl. Jesus has both forgiven you of your sins and freed you from the power of sin in your life. But, for as long as you are on earth, you will still have to battle sin, and you will sometimes still sin.

What exactly is sin? Sin can be defined as an action, failure to act, motive, or attitude that is not consistent with God's holy nature or commandments. When you are His girl, sin hinders but does not cut off your fellowship with God. To pursue a healthy and growing relationship with Him, you want to seek growth in turning away from sin with the Lord's help.

Ask the Lord to show you the sin in your life that is hindering your relationship with Him. When the Holy Spirit convicts you of sin, you can:

- recognize it.
- confess it to Jesus and ask and receive His forgiveness.
- turn from it by His power and walk towards Him by His grace.

For example, the Lord could convict you of thinking unkind

thoughts about someone. You could recognize and admit it as sin, confess it to Him from your heart, receive His forgiveness, and turn from it by His power to walk with obedience to Him by His grace! You could pray something like, "Jesus, I realize that I have been thinking unkind thoughts about this person, and that was wrong. I know it grieves You. I confess it to You, seek to turn from it with Your help, and ask You to help me walk in Your grace to think thoughts that are honoring to You!"

You will need to do this throughout your life on earth – and it is an incredible thing! It is a reminder of your constant need for Jesus, of the beauty of the Gospel, and is a cause to worship Him for His grace.

It is so helpful for you to understand the difference between conviction and condemnation. The Holy Spirit will bring conviction of sin that brings with it grace to turn from that sin and walk in His ways! The enemy seeks to bring condemnation that leaves you lying in guilt and feeling like there is no hope.

Know that Jesus is by your side in this growth process and delights in helping you take the next step!

This is so important to remember: the closer you get to Jesus, the more you will see your sin and need for Jesus. This allows you to grow more and come to more freedom and joy! Just like the closer you get to the light, the more you can see dirt – and seek for it to be cleaned away.

You see, sin may sparkle for a moment, but you will find that it only ultimately brings damage. Understand that while Jesus forgives and takes away the punishment, the reality of sin is that it will hurt you and has real consequences. You want to avoid it as much as possible! Run from it like you would from a fierce tiger. Love Jesus and the joy of thriving in Him more than any sin in your life!

127

1 John 1:8-9 gives us this truth – *"If we say we have no sin, we deceive ourselves and the Truth is not in us, but if we confess our sin, He is faithful and just, to forgive us our sin and to cleanse us from all unrighteousness."*

Isn't that beautiful? It is a supernatural work, and you can look to Jesus to do it!

Growing Pains

Let's talk about growing pains. Sometimes in this growth process, you will experience growing pains. Growth in Jesus is not always comfortable, but it is worth it! He works in us, and if it hurts, it is a good hurt. He is removing sin from your life and making you more like Jesus. It is like the good-for-you pain of a surgeon cutting to remove a disease.

For example, He could allow you to walk through a humbling situation, to clean pride from your heart. He does it because He loves you and wants your best. (See Hebrews 12:5-11.) Lean into Jesus and His work in you. Do not run from it – knowing He is working it for His glory and your good!

It is an issue of choosing your pain – either the short and worthwhile pain of Jesus working to help you to thrive more or the lasting pain of staying where you are and missing out on what Jesus has for you! *"Therefore as you have received Christ Jesus the Lord, so walk in Him, having been firmly rooted and now being built up in Him and established in your faith, just as you were instructed, and overflowing with gratitude."* (Colossians 2:6-7)

The Beauty of Grace

The Lord's grace is so beautiful! His grace is what saves you, empowers you to grow in Him, and covers you when you fall short. Isn't grace amazing? Listen to these encouraging verses:

"For by grace you have been saved through faith. And this is not your own doing; it is the gift of God..." (Ephesians 2:8)

"For from his fullness we have all received, grace upon grace." (John 1:16)

"...My grace is sufficient for you, for my power is made perfect in weakness.' Therefore I will boast all the more gladly of my weaknesses, so that the power of Christ may rest upon me." (2 Corinthians 12:9)

"In him we have redemption through his blood, the forgiveness of our trespasses, according to the riches of his grace..." (Ephesians 1:7)

Grace is not something you earn, but something you receive that transforms you! The grace Jesus extended to you is not an excuse to sin on purpose. A true understanding of grace will cause you to worship Jesus, and seek to walk in His grace, which empowers you to grow in, obey, and follow Him.

Growth and Not Perfection

It is so important to see that He is after your growth and not your perfection. You can never be perfect on your own – that is why you need a Savior. Jesus is perfect on your behalf. Then, He grows you to become more like Him for His glory and your good. Do you see the big difference?

The Goal

Remember the goal! Jesus is growing you, working in your heart, bringing transformation – and blossoming you to increasingly thrive in what you were created for in Him as His girl! The goal is to become like your Jesus, thrive in Him, and live a life that shines with Jesus more and more. The more Jesus grows you, the greater the joy. This results in His glory! He will fulfill His goal! Like a master craftsman working with their mind set on the goal, the Lord keeps working to fulfill His goal. *"But by the grace of God I am what I am, and his grace toward me was not in vain…"* (1 Corinthians 15:10)

One Practical Step to Take

I encourage you to look at one choice you need to make today and to apply the "Power Question" to it, asking, "Will this help me grow in Jesus, or pull me away from Him?"

The thing I am asking the "Power Question" about today is:

_____

_____

_____

The answer to the question is:

_____

_____

_____

Watch how the Lord guides you!

It is a Lifelong Process — and Privilege

For as long as you live on this earth, Jesus will continue to work and make you more like Himself. It is a day-by-day thing – a process. Do not be discouraged if you do not instantly grow very much! It can be easy to wish that you could drink an "Instant Growth" shake and suddenly grow a lot, can't it? But Jesus has a purpose in the process! He keeps you dependent on Him, meets you in the growth, and does beautiful things. It is an amazing, life-long process! Just like you cannot expect a baby to start walking in a day or a plant to produce fruit in a moment, so your growth in Jesus takes time. He is not finished with you!

There may be seasons where you cannot feel or see the growth, but He is working big time! It is like a seed growing beneath the surface, ready to bloom. Continue to receive His grace to press into Jesus and embrace growth through the tools He has given. Fruit will come for you as His girl! You can watch as He faithfully does the work in your life, transforming you more and more into His likeness! *"He has made everything beautiful in its time…"* (Ecclesiastes 3:11)

Growing in Jesus

Jesus will be faithful to complete the work that He began in you. Insert your name here:

> "…He who began a good work in you, _____, will bring it to completion at the day of Jesus Christ." (Philippians 1:6)

You can respond to Him in prayer with something like this: "Jesus, thank You for making me Yours and for beginning a work in me of growing me by Your Spirit. I pray that You would help me to embrace You and Your work in me!" He delights to answer.

The closer you get to Jesus, the more He makes you like Him, the more He shines from your life, and the more joy and fruits of the Spirit you experience in your life! You will increasingly thrive in the way Jesus created you to in your life in Him, as His girl. It is so worth it! Can you see this? Growing is an amazing gift!

Go embrace Jesus and this growth in Him by His Spirit, and watch the beautiful fruit He brings in your heart and life! ⋘

STUDY GUIDE

What was one thing that was especially helpful to you in this chapter?

_____

_____

_____

What is one step that you will take today to apply it to your own life?

_____

_____

What is one struggle that you face in this area that you can ask Jesus to help you overcome?

_____

_____

Look up these Bible verses and write what Jesus shows you:

- 2 Corinthians 3:18

_____

_____

- Colossians 2:6-7

_____

_____

_____

- Philippians 1:6

_____

_____

_____

Pray or write out a prayer of response to Jesus.

_____

_____

_____

_____

Write the Focus Statement for this chapter.

_____

_____

_____

You can write any additional thoughts here.

_____

_____

_____

_____

focus statement

LIVE AS HIS
with Christ
as your life

CHAPTER 7

Living as His Girl

AUTHENTICALLY LIVING AS CHRIST'S GIRL BY THE POWER OF HIS LIFE IN YOU

"For to me to live is Christ..." (Philippians 1:21)

....

What — or who — are you living for?

What – or who – is your life about?

As Christ's girl, you have the privilege of authentically living out of love for Jesus as His girl – in Him, from the realities of Him and His Truth in your life, and for Him – empowered by His Spirit in you, for His glory. As you do, you will experience more and more of Jesus and the life you were created for in Him as His girl!

What Living as His Girl Is

Stretch! You wake up in the morning. The Lord has given you another day to live. You put your feet on the floor and you personally have the call, gift, and joy of living with, in, and for Jesus today – by the power of His life in you. You are His. You have life in Christ, His life in you, and a beautiful purpose to live with the One Who gave you life – Jesus! He has given you physical life, eternal life in Him, a reason to live, and a message of His eternal life to share! Isn't that so amazing? That is something to get you excited for the day!

Listen to this: *"...He died for all, that those who live might no longer live for themselves but for him who for their sake died and was raised."* (2 Corinthians 5:15)

> *This is the amazing place where Truth connects with and comes out in how you live your everyday life!*

This is the amazing place where "the rubber meets the road" and Truth meets living. Where Who He is to you, what is true in His Word, what He has done in you, and what He has called and empowered you to do by the Holy Spirit – connects with and comes out in how you live your real, everyday life! It is where your walk and talk collide, and you see what is real. It is easy to say that you believe something, but the real evidence is when you live it, and your life shows it, right? Let's dive in!

Why This Life Is So Important

Are you wondering why actually living this life is so important? Living this life is so important because it is the life you were created for in Jesus. It is the outflow of the life and the realities you have received in Him as His girl. As you live by the power of the Spirit, it results in you fulfilling your purpose of glorifying Him! It is important to understand that you must personally live this life in Jesus step-by-step in your real life. *"...Christ who is your life..."* (Colossians 3:4) Just like you can take your place at the beginning of a race track, but it is only as you personally take steps that you are actually running the race. So, you must actually live this life as His girl in daily, moment-by-moment life!

A Glimpse of What This Life Looks Like

So, what can this life look like? Let's get a glimpse! While there is so much more in the Bible to see, this will give you a start. We will catch a glimpse here, and then unpack in more detail, ways that you can live out this life! Does that sound good?

It is a life that:

≫ **Is lived all about Jesus** – He is the focus of your life, your all, what your life is about, and where your life points! *"I have been crucified with Christ, nevertheless I live, yet not I, but, Christ lives in me, and the life I now live, I live by faith in the Son of God who loved me and gave Himself for me."* (Galatians 2:20)

≫ **Is lived out of gratitude, love, and worship** – You live out of gratitude, love, and worship of the One Who saved you, made you His forever, and has given you this life He made you to live in Him! *"I appeal to you therefore, brothers, by the mercies of God, to present your bodies as a living sacrifice, holy and acceptable to God, which is your spiritual worship."* (Romans 12:1)

≫ **Knows she is His girl and lives in that security, joy, and purpose** – *"...You are Christ's..."* (1 Corinthians 3:23)

≫ **Lives like you are His girl** – *"...He died for all, that those who live might no longer live for themselves but* for him who for their sake died and was raised." (2 Corinthians 5:15)

≫ **Embraces the call** – To live from what you know and believe of the realities from His Word – including the realities that are yours in Jesus as His girl! *"...Be doers of the word, and not hearers only..."* (James 1:22)

≫ **Is empowered by His Life** – the Holy Spirit in you – not your own strength – *"...Not by might, nor by power, but by my Spirit, says the LORD of hosts."* (Zechariah 4:6)

≫ **Is lived with an eternal perspective** – *"...We look not to the things that are seen but to the things that are unseen. For the things that are seen are transient, but the things that are unseen are eternal."* (2 Corinthians 4:8)

≫ **Is lived like Heaven is home** – *"Do not lay up for yourselves treasures on earth, where moth and rust destroy and where thieves break in and steal, but lay up for yourselves treasures in heaven, where neither moth nor rust destroys and where thieves do not break in and steal. For where your treasure is, there your heart will be also."* (Matthew 6:19-21)

≫ **Is lived for His glory** – *"...That in everything he might be preeminent."* (Colossians 1:18)

This is just the beginning! It is a peek into the powerful life you are meant to live as His girl! Isn't this exciting and amazing?

A Life Only Explainable by Jesus

This incredible life is a life that cannot be explained, except for Jesus and His transforming life and work in and through you! It is impossible any other way. Jesus desires to make every moment of your life filled with His life – from the little to the big things! If you try to live the life Jesus created you for and called you to in your own strength, you will find that you cannot do it, and will exhaust yourself trying.

This keeps you close to and dependent on Him! As you do, people will see the results in your life – for example: of your joy and servant heart – and know this is not normal. It points to the source of your life – Jesus. And this is the beautiful thing about life this way – you are freed and empowered, God is glorified, and others are offered hope! *"...Christ in you, the hope of glory."* (Colossians 1:27) Let's remember these verses again: *"Not that we are sufficient of ourselves... our sufficiency is from God..."* (2 Corinthians 3:5) *"...Not by might, nor by power, but by my Spirit, says the LORD of hosts."* (Zechariah 4:6) This is so beautiful! The only explanation for your life is Jesus! Can you see this?

The Impact in Your Life

Living as His girl has a powerful impact in your life! I have found so much joy, purpose, security, and life in living as His girl – by the power of His Spirit in me! I would not trade it for anything. It is truly living. You can experience it, too!

Can you picture the impact in your life? This could look like walking through your day, believing the realities from His Word that are yours as His girl (like you saw a glimpse of above). As you do, you will experience the impact of it in your own life – including joy and purpose! Actually living in a reality personally brings amazing results that you will experience for yourself – as you live in it by the power of the Holy Spirit in you! It is like a gazelle knowing it was given amazing speed and freedom to run, moving its legs, running through the field, and experiencing the wonder of it.

The impact of living out of Jesus' life within you brings these things:

⤞ Purpose and meaning

⤞ Joy, freedom, and peace

⫸ Transformation

⫸ Guidance

⫸ Living a life that's only explanation is Jesus

⫸ Impact on others for Him

⫸ Eternal impact and building His eternal Kingdom

⫸ Glory to God

⫸ And more!

You will experience Jesus in new ways and the fruit of Him in and through your life. As you live your life for Jesus, and Jesus lives through you, others will see Jesus real in your life, see the fruit in your life, and some will be inspired to do the same. Your life is always having an impact on everyone around you – for good or for bad! Living this life as His girl will impact you and others for His glory! It is so exciting! There is so much more impact in and through your life that you will personally discover as you live as His girl in real life!

Like we saw in the chapter on becoming His girl, this is so true:

"If anyone would come after me, let him deny himself and take up his cross and follow me. For whoever would save his life, will lose it, but whoever loses his life for my sake will find it. For what will it profit a man if he gains the whole world and forfeits his soul? Or what shall a man give in exchange for his soul?" (Matthew 16:24-26)

This is when you are truly alive. This is when you truly begin to live – when you become His, believe the Truth of His Word, and live for Jesus by the power of His life in you. This is living! This life as His girl compares to no other!

How to Live as His Girl

How do you live as His girl? It is a moment-by-moment calling and privilege that you have the joy of walking and growing in every day of your life!

While there are many, some powerful ways to live as His girl include:

Look to Him for His help and depend on Him in the Spirit – to live a Spirit-empowered life by – His life in you. This life in Jesus as His is a life only possible by His life being lived in and through you! Living as His requires depending on Him and His Spirit to empower you to follow Him step by step. Listen to this beautiful verse once again, *"...Not by might, nor by power, but by my Spirit, says the LORD of hosts."* (Zechariah 4:6) You are empowered by His Life – the Holy Spirit in you – not by your own strength. Ask Him for His help, and step forward in faith, depending on the Holy Spirit for all you need to live as His girl. As He empowers you, you can live a life only possible by Him!

Focus on your relationship with Jesus and the state of your heart as key – your life flows from your heart. Both you personally, and your living, are impacted by your relationship with the Lord and your heart. Remember this powerful verse, *"Keep your heart with all vigilance, for from it flow the springs of life."* (Proverbs 4:23) A transformed heart results in transformed living! You do not want to just change your actions, in the way you live on the outside, with no heart change. You want a transformed heart that flows out in how you live. Right? The more you grow in your relationship with Jesus, and He changes your heart, the more your life will reflect it – becoming more like Jesus and the life He created you for as His girl!

Rest in being His. What a matchless gift! *"...You are Christ's..."* (1 Corinthians 3:23) Rest in this instead of looking for rest in other things that can never give true rest. This will bring you inner joy, confidence, and peace!

Live in and from the realities that are yours in Jesus as His girl in faith – what you know and truly believe. Live knowing the truths are real, believing them, and living them out in your daily life – a life of faith in Jesus and His Word! We will look at this more in a special section below!

Live Jesus – as He lives in you – do not just talk about Him. Live the reality of Him in your everyday life. Live in Him, with Him, and Him through you!

Live saying "Yes" to Jesus in anything He asks of you – it is essentially living a "Yes" to Jesus. As His girl, He always has your "Yes." Live for Jesus and not yourself or anyone else. This is a joy! It is like living for a rescuer. If there was someone who saved your physical life, you would be so grateful, and want to do whatever you could to bless them, right?

Live as His — "I am Christ's girl!" — in your mindset, heart state, and practical daily life.

It is living as His – "I am Christ's girl!" – in your mindset, heart state, and practical daily life (in your thoughts, choices, actions, etc.). It is looking into His Word, the Bible, and saying, "Yes!" Jesus says, *"If you love me, you will keep my commandments."* (John 14:15) You prove your love for Jesus when you obey Him. Obedience to Jesus and His Word is your call as His girl!

Do it when it is a joy, and do it when you do not want to, feel like it, or find joy in obeying. It means saying "Yes" to Jesus, wherever you are right now. It is saying "Yes" in living for Him in this moment, seeking to obey what you read in His Word, turning away from sin, etc. Here is the beautiful thing – you know His love, His heart, and that whatever He calls you to do, is for your good and His glory! As you live as His girl, Jesus should always have your "Yes." If you do so, there is no end to what He will do!

Do all that you do for Jesus. *"...Whatever you do, do all to the glory of God."* (1 Corinthians 10:31) When you do what you do for

Jesus, it is never lost – no matter how big or small, or how people respond. Doing what you do for Jesus, and out of love for Him, is beautiful!

Live for His Kingdom. As His girl, you are called to be living for Jesus' eternal Kingdom. You want your life to be about Him and His Kingdom – and not about the kingdom of this world, or building your own kingdom about yourself! *"Jesus answered, 'My kingdom is not of this world...'"* (John 18:36) We will look more at how you can do this in the *Serving and Sharing Jesus* chapter.

Keep an eternal perspective. You know and live like your life is not just about this immediate life on earth, but about the eternal life to come! *"...As we look not to the things that are seen but to the things that are unseen. For the things that are seen are transient, but the things that are unseen are eternal."* (2 Corinthians 4:18) As you live with an eternal perspective – living your life in light of eternity – it will compel you to invest your life in what matters and will last forever.

What will last forever? Your relationship with Jesus and peoples' souls. When you know the reality that every human soul will live forever in eternity, it will change how you see things. For example, when you see cars driving past you, you will not just see cars, you will see cars containing people with souls headed for an eternal destiny. This then changes how you live in investing in growing in your own relationship with Jesus and in pointing others to Him. When this life is over, it is just the beginning of eternal life with Jesus in Heaven for all who are His! How could you live in light of eternity today? This is so powerful!

Live like Heaven is your Home. Heaven is your true home. This earth is not your home. When life on earth is over, it is just the beginning of eternal life with Jesus in Heaven! Heaven is where Jesus is, where He has prepared a place for you, and where you will live with Him forever in eternity! Isn't that so incredible?

As you believe and live your story in this reality, it gives you so much peace and purpose. Live like your true home is not here on earth, but in Heaven with Jesus. *"Do not lay up for yourselves treasures on earth, where moth and rust destroy and where thieves break in and steal, but lay up for yourselves treasures in heaven, where neither moth nor rust destroys and where thieves do not break in and steal. For where your treasure is, there your heart will be also."* (Matthew 6:19-21)

Be ready to die for your Jesus. *"For to me, to live is Christ, and to die is gain."* (Philippians 1:21) You are in an amazing place because either you get to live with, by, and for Him – or you get to go be with Him in Heaven! You have something worth living for when you have something worth dying for. We are all called to give our lives daily in serving Jesus. You may be called to give your life – to die – for Jesus in standing for His name. Live ready to die for the One Who gave His life for you and gave eternal life to you! Live a life that says, "Jesus is what life is about, wonderful, and worth all I am." Listen to this beautiful verse, *"For if we live, we live to the Lord, and if we die, we die to the Lord. So then, whether we live or whether we die, we are the Lord's."* (Romans 14:8)

Let your life be all about Jesus. *"...To live is Christ..."* (Philippians 1:21) Live a life wrapped up in Christ. Let Him be the focus of your life, your all, what your life is about, and what your life points to. A life that says, "Jesus is not just part of my life – He is my life." *"...Christ, who is your life..."* (Colossians 3:4) It is a daily, moment-by-moment living in Jesus, with Jesus, filled with Jesus, by His Spirit, and empowered by Jesus. It is living for Jesus by Him living through you! It is so real. When Jesus is your life and it is all about Him, it is good – no matter what you face – because you always have Him, and He is always good! It is living as a girl who loves Jesus. No other way of living compares!

Live for His glory. Live seeking to lift Jesus up, in every area of your life! It is a life that says – "I am His – and He is so good!" It is a life of worship. You have the joy of looking to Jesus and pointing people to Him and His matchless goodness! *"...That in everything he might be preeminent."* (Colossians 1:18)

As you pursue living as His girl, remember this powerful verse, *"For the love of Christ controls us, because we have concluded this: that one has died for all, therefore all have died; and he died for all, that those who live might no longer live for themselves but for him who for their sake died and was raised."* (2 Corinthians 5:14-15) Isn't that beautiful? It is a life controlled by love for Jesus that lives for Him – the One Who gave His life for you and gave you life!

Throughout your life, you will always be growing in living as His. It is a lifelong process and joy — empowered by His Spirit in you!

Throughout your whole life, you will always be growing in living as His. It is a lifelong process and joy of walking and thriving more and more into this living – empowered by His Spirit in you!

As you live, remember this: *"...You are Christ's..."* (1 Corinthians 3:23)

Making Choices in Line with Being His Girl

You are constantly facing choices every day, aren't you? Choices make up your life. These choices include how you spend your time, who you have as friends, things you do for entertainment, where you go, what you do, how you spend your money, what comes out of your life, what you say, what you think, and what you watch, listen to, look at, or read!

As you make your choices, you want to make them in line with being His, what He calls you to in His Word, and what is consistent with Who He is. You want your heart's motive in making your choices to be love, obedience, and honor for Jesus. So, in real, practical life, what does this look like? Let's imagine you are wondering if you should read a certain book, or watch a certain movie, or listen to a certain song. You can ask, "Will this help me live for, follow, and glorify Jesus?"

For example, ask this question when making specific choices like choosing to listen to music. Will it help you grow in your love for Jesus or fill your mind with lies that will do the opposite? Or, ask it for the daily things in your life like meeting a friend for coffee – which either can or cannot help you know, grow in, and follow Jesus.

Will this help me live for, follow, and glorify Jesus?

Your personal interaction with Jesus can be to ask Him, "Jesus, do You want me to do this?" What He shows you will be guided by the Holy Spirit and will always match with God's Word. Listen to this powerful verse, *"...Whatever you do, do all to the glory of God."* (1 Corinthians 10:31) This means in every area of your life. Ask yourself, "Can I do this for the glory of God – lifting Jesus up – here?" This helps!

Another helpful question is – "Would I watch, listen, read, say, or do this if Jesus were in the room with me?" This is a good question to remind you that Jesus is always right there with you. If you still wonder what to do, ask a godly mentor. If you still are in doubt, it is better to not. You love Him and you want to do what honors Him. You do not do something just to be a "good girl!" You know Jesus is always calling you to what is for His greatest glory, your truest best, and the most blessing to others. You can trust Him. It is such a safe place! This will help you so much as you make your choices!

So, insert something you need to make a choice on in this question: "Will _____ (whatever the thing you are making the choice on) help me to know, follow, and live for Jesus?"

The Desert Island Test

Another helpful and fun way to make choices is to do the Desert Island Test! Imagine making your choice as if you were on a desert island, all alone with only Jesus and your Bible. What would be the right thing to do? You do not have a culture telling you what is popular or acceptable. You only have God showing you what to do. Live in line with what He shows you. What is popular or culturally acceptable is always changing – like side ponytails, moral decisions, etc. But, Jesus and His Word never change. Is that helpful?

It is like an athlete preparing for a big event makes every choice in line with what will help them reach their goal – what to eat, how much sleep to get, the amount of exercise to do, etc. In the same way, you want to make choices in line with what will help you reach the goal of Jesus and living the life He created you for in Him as His girl!

These are some helpful tools in making choices. The main thing is to look to Jesus and His Word and let Him guide you to make the choices that He has called you to make!

Living Out Your Faith

What would your life look like if you really believed what Jesus said? Like we have touched on previously, there is such power when you look at the truth of His Word, believe it, and then, live in and from the reality of it. You take Jesus at His Word – and live it out in faith! Live like the Truth is real. Let that transform how you think, live, talk, act, and make choices. Ask Jesus to take it from your head to your heart in a way that transforms your heart, flows out in the way that you live, and lifts Him up to others! This truth you live out in faith is everything that Jesus has told you in His Word, the Bible.

Some of the realities of truth from His Word that are yours as His girl and that you can live in light of include:

⟫ You are His!
⟫ Jesus is real and is Who He says He is!
⟫ His Word is true!
⟫ You are who He says you are!
⟫ What He has called you to is your purpose!
⟫ His Spirit is empowering you!
⟫ Your home is Heaven!
⟫ Eternity is forever!
⟫ His glory is your goal!
⟫ ...And more from the Bible!

Remember you live what you truly believe. You can say with your mouth that what you have heard or think is true, but how you live is proof of what you really believe. Let's look at how this will work!

For example, you could say:

> "Jesus, You are _____ (a reality about who Jesus is). I am _____ (a reality about your identity in Jesus) in You. You say _____ (a reality from His Word) is true in Your Word. So, I will live like it is true." ("I will live in it, from it, and by it.")

How would your life change if you lived like these realities were really true? Pause and ask yourself – "What would my life look like if I truly believed what Jesus said is true?" How would living in faith change your life? If you live placing your faith and trust in Jesus, walking in faith, and living life believing Jesus, the results flow out in your life. What can you imagine the results being in your life? It has the power to be life-changing. *"...Be doers of the word, and not hearers only..."* (James 1:22)

So, let's look at examples:

Live for and in light of eternity. When you know that eternity is real, it impacts how you do daily things. It does not mean you never do things such as coffee with a friend. But what you do, you do with an eternal perspective! What is your purpose and goal in doing that thing? Will it help you know Him or share Him? Will it refresh you, so you are more energized to serve Him? You live in the beautiful and sobering reality of eternity!

Live like your body is a temple of the Holy Spirit. When you know that your body is a temple of the Holy Spirit, it will impact what you do with it, right? *"Or do you not know that your body is a temple of the Holy Spirit within you, whom you have from God? You are not your own, for you were bought with a price. So glorify God in your body."* (1 Corinthians 6:19-20)

Do you see how this works? Now you try filling it in:

"Jesus, You are _____. I am _____ in You. You say _____ is true in Your Word. So, I will live like it is true."

It is like looking through a glasses lens – where you see life through the lens of what you know and believe about Who Jesus is, what He says is true in His Word, who you are in Jesus, what you are called to, where your true home is, and the power you are called to live through in the Holy Spirit. Then you go live in the reality of it! You are talking the talk and walking the walk. You are walking in and living out your faith in real life! Receive His grace to live in these realities, and watch Him change your life!

Living a Life in Him That is Real, Authentic, and Genuine

It is so powerful for you to be the real deal. You need for both your mouth and life to say, "I need Jesus. He is the answer to my need. I still struggle and His grace covers me, picks me up, and strengthens me. No one compares to my Jesus, and no life compares to life in Him. He and this life in Him are amazing!" This glorifies Jesus, brings joy to you, and offers hope to others. It is a life of joy, confidence, and humility. There is no faking, performing, or pretending. It is not saying, "I have it all together," but, "I have Jesus." and "You can have Him, too." We are all hungry for something that is real — I am, you are, and the world is. This is real. It is the real deal! A real Christian life. This is transforming life! Let us live it by His life in us!

This kind of genuine living points not to our goodness, but to the goodness of the One Who is satisfying us and transforming our lives — Jesus!

Are you perfect? No.

Is the One you belong to, Who lives in you, and Who shines through you perfect? Yes.

He is your hope, not you. When you fail, you run to Him for grace. When you triumph, it is because of His grace working in your life. It is about Him. It is His life in you. It is His life through you. That is the beautiful thing. It is about Him!

I can say this personally. I am not perfect. I need Jesus desperately every moment. And I have Him. I need all my hope in Him. I want to point others to Him and His goodness with my life.

Friend, this kind of genuine living points not to our goodness, but to the goodness of the One Who is satisfying us and transforming our lives — Jesus! Jesus is real; You can live authentically the life that He created you for in Him. Real living points to a real Savior, Who offers real hope. That is what we all need!

Embracing a Life That is Faithful to Jesus and What He Has Called You To

It is so powerful to embrace the life that is faithful to Jesus! Let's look at some ways.

Embrace the life that Jesus has called you to live. This transforms your life! Your life will look different! This kind of living is the outflow of a new heart and a desire to follow Jesus, empowered by His Spirit. It is not performing out of fear to earn God's favor, but because you have His favor in Jesus, and you do it out of love for Him and a reverence for His holiness. You do it because you know He made you, knows what is best for you, and all that He calls you to is for your good.

It is heart transformation to personal holiness as He works in you. This results in living and obedience consistent with His Word, empowered by the Spirit, for His glory. Your life will be in line more and more with what Jesus has called you to, who He has called you to be, how He has called you to live, and what He has called you to do. It will be a life lived from a transformed heart that is motivated out of love for, joy in, and desire to honor Jesus!

Be willing to be faithful to and do what Jesus calls you to no matter what. You see, as you are His and follow Him, sometimes people will not understand — and you will feel alone, be made fun of, or be left out. Although it can be hard, you know that it is all worth it. It is like wearing a life jacket because you know your ship is going to sink, and everyone makes fun of you. You would know it was worth it — whether people understood and embraced it or did not and made fun of you. Right? The most important thing is to be faithful to Jesus and what He has shown you to do in His Word!

Live in faithfulness to Him, and His call, in a way of living that says, "I love Jesus, and I want to honor Him." Do not have an "I am better than you" spirit. Say to Jesus, "I will live for You no matter what!" Know what you believe and why you are doing what you are doing – like you saw in the *A Girl of Word* chapter! Stand up for what you know Jesus has called you to do, out of love for Jesus, with humility and confidence.

Be who He has called you to be at all times. Do not be a certain way on Sunday mornings, another way, with a group of friends, and another way by yourself. When you try to fit in to be accepted or have friends, it can lead you to do things that are wrong or are not smart.

Be who Jesus has called you to be, and stick with what you know is right. The right people will be attracted to you, and you will inspire them to do the same. If some choose to no longer be your friend because you are being faithful to Jesus, they are not the kind of friends you want. It is better to be faithful to Jesus than to do what is wrong.

Remember you are living with and before Jesus right now. You will stand before Jesus someday and give an account for how you lived – without any of the people there who ridiculed you for doing right or tried to influence you to do wrong. It is powerful to live for Him alone and to hear Him say, "...*Well done, good and faithful servant...*" (Matthew 25:23)

Live a life that is not like the world but like Jesus. Live life in pursuit of Jesus and what He has called you to. Do not look to the world for its example, or walk in its ways that are founded on the flesh. This world does not have the hope of Christ, and is looking for hope and fulfillment in things other than Jesus that can never satisfy. It is important to clarify that some things – for example, styles, activities, etc., are okay if they honor Jesus, but the mindset of the world, and the things that flow from it, are what you want to guard against. You are here to be a light; not to blend in. Live as Christ's girl who lives in the world, but is not of the world. *"Do not love the world or the things in the world. If anyone loves the world, the love of the Father is not in him. For all that is in the world – the desires of the flesh and the desires of the eyes and pride of life – is not from the Father but is from the world. And the world is passing away along with its desires, but whoever does the will of God abides forever."* (1 John 2:15-17)

These things are so powerful as you live as His girl!

Grace for Every Moment

Like we looked at before, grace is what saves you, empowers you to live for Him, and is what picks you up when you fall. Jesus gives you grace for every moment of your life and for all He calls you to do. Look to Him, ask Him for, and receive His grace for this moment and day. *"Let us then with confidence draw near to the throne of grace, that we may receive mercy and find grace to help in time of need."* (Hebrews 4:16)

A Powerful Help in Living as His— True Friendship and Relationship

Do you like having friends? I know I do! While Jesus is all that you truly need, He has given you a great gift in human relationships to encourage and help you grow in Him and this life in Him. He designed you to live in community – in connection – with others. To be cheered on in your walk with Him by others who are walking with Him, too. It is so important to have friendships where you point each other to Jesus and cheer one another on in Him and the journey with Him. Let's look at different kinds of relationships that are so powerful and can be a big encouragement in your walk with Jesus and your life in Him!

These include:

A mentor – Look for someone who has a walk with Jesus that you admire (who is not perfect but genuine), who is ahead of you in their walk with the Lord, and who can encourage you in your walk with the Lord. (This mentor relationship can be a parent, a godly woman at church, an older girl who walks with Jesus, etc.)

A companion – Seek out someone who is at a similar place in their walk with the Lord so you can walk together on this journey with Jesus. Someone with whom you can mutually cheer each other on in your walks with Him.

A mentee – Watch for someone who is younger than you in their faith and whom you can encourage in their walk with Jesus.

A community – Find true community through a church, small group, Bible study, etc., where you can seek Jesus together and encourage one another in Him.

> "…Exhort one another every day, as long as it is called 'today,' that none of you may be hardened by the deceitfulness of sin."
> (Hebrews 3:13)

Do you see the gift these relationships can be and how they will impact your life?

Having these different kinds of relationships is so powerful in your life. If there is no one in your area, you can find someone long-distance and connect by phone. It is important – if at all possible – to have someone who truly knows you and can walk through life with you.

A word on guy relationships – Seek to encourage one another in Christ as brothers and sisters in Jesus in purity and joy. He will bring the right man into your life in His time and purpose if it is His will for you to marry. You can trust the Lord for this! Be a good sister in Jesus, and at the right time, if it is His will, He will bring the right man – someone with whom you can follow Jesus with all of your life! Do not settle for someone with whom you cannot follow Jesus!

A word on ministry or missionary relationships – It is good to share Jesus with those who do not know Him and make an impact on them for Him. Just be sure that the Lord is impacting them through you, and they are not having a negative impact on or drawing you away from your relationship with Jesus. You can ask your parents or a godly mentor to help you be aware of this! Watch the depth and influence of these outreach relationships on you. Your closest friendships should be with those who are His girls because you share the most important thing in life. Seek the Lord for the right balance!

It is so important to have friendships where you point each other to Jesus and cheer one another on in your journeys with Him.

It is so important to choose your friends wisely. Make sure that you are encouraging each other closer to Jesus as you are living as His girl and are not hurting your relationship with Him! It just takes one friend to pull you closer to Jesus or to damage your relationship with Him. Seek His grace to see and step away from relationships that damage your relationship with Him. It is far better to have a small number of friends who encourage you in Jesus than to have a lot of friends who do not encourage you in Jesus!

Ask the Lord to provide these relationships for you, keep your eyes open, pursue these relationships, and see how He uses them to encourage you both in your relationship with Him! This is a beautiful gift from Jesus! *"Iron sharpens iron, and one man sharpens another."* (Proverbs 17:17)

Ask yourself:

Who are my closest friends?

Are we encouraging each other towards Jesus?

Who am I walking through life with?

Who am I allowing to mentor and impact me?

Like a wolf drawing a lone sheep away from the flock, the enemy wants to isolate you, make you feel alone in your journey, your longing for Jesus, and your struggle with sin – and try to drag you down and away from Jesus. The Lord has given us each other to encourage one another in Him.

He could have put us alone on an island. But He gave us each other. The Bible talks about the friendship of David and Jonathan and that this is what Jonathan did for David, "...*strengthened his hand in God.*" (1 Samuel 23:16) Let's do that for each other!

Seek to pursue and embrace these friendships and relationships that will encourage you and them in Jesus and in living for Him as His own. Watch what the Lord will do!

Things That Can Hold You Back

As you excitedly seek to live as His girl, there will be things that try to hold you back! It is good to be aware of them, watch for them, and deal with them – so they do not get in the way of living as fully as possible as His!

These obstacles can include:

- ⤜ Distractions with other things
- ⤜ Doubts
- ⤜ Sin and disobedience
- ⤜ Laziness
- ⤜ Lack of time in the Word and fellowship with people who love Jesus
- ⤜ Relationships that pull you away from Jesus
- ⤜ Fear of people and what they will think
- ⤜ Self-focus
- ⤜ The enemy
- ⤜ And more!

What do you feel is holding you back from living as His girl? Write a few of the things here:

For example, an obstacle could be getting distracted with entertainment or projects you want to do and finding that you are living for yourself instead of Jesus. Confess it to Jesus and ask for His help to overcome it! You can also talk with a friend or mentor and ask for prayer!

Listen to these amazing Bible verses:

> *"If we confess our sins, he is faithful and just to forgive us our sins and to cleanse us from all unrighteousness."* (1 John 1:9)

"...Let us also lay aside every weight, and sin which clings so closely, and let us run with endurance the race that is set before us." (Hebrews 12:1)

"So flee youthful passions and pursue righteousness, faith, love, and peace, along with those who call on the Lord from a pure heart." (2 Timothy 2:22)

He is greater than any struggle that you face! *"...He who is in you is greater than he who is in the world."* (1 John 4:4) Seek to strengthen yourself against that area of struggle through a verse from the Bible and the "Growth Tools" that Jesus works through to strengthen you in Him!

It is worth it! Nothing is worth holding you back. This life is what you were made for as His girl!

A Call to Action

Experience and live this for yourself! It is vibrant living! It is a life where you face the day with Jesus and live by faith. *"...The righteous shall live by faith."* (Galatians 3:11) To say to Jesus – in faith, "This is Who You are, this is who I am in You, this is what is true, this is what You have called me to do through the power of Your life in me – and I am Yours. I believe You, I say "Yes" to You, I live for You from these Truths by Your life in me, and I believe that I will experience the amazing fruit for Your glory." And then step out to live in it by the power of His life in you. This is a transformed, vibrant, and supernatural life only possible by Jesus. You will see the incredible results that He brings! It is meant to be yours!

Live in the realities that are yours as His girl, by the power of His Spirit, for His glory!

Your life in Jesus:

It says – "I'm His!"

It is empowered by His life in you.

It lives from the realities that are yours in Him and the transformed heart He has given you.

It points to Him.

It radiates His goodness.

A life that says, "...to live is Christ..."! (Philippians 1:21) A life that fulfills your true purpose – to know and glorify Him as His girl!

An Application Step

Ask yourself: "What is one thing I can say 'yes' to Jesus in today?" Write it here:

_____

_____

_____

Then seek to go do it by His grace!

A Personal Call

You are called – and blessed – to live as His girl! This is His promise that you will find life here: "...Whoever would save his life, will lose it, but whoever loses his life for my sake will find it." (Matthew 16:25) This is your call to go live as His girl from the realities that are yours as His girl, by the power of His Spirit in you, and for His glory!

Seek to live a life of purpose, joy, and transformation – a life of Jesus – that is only explainable by Him! "...To live is Christ..." (Philippians 1:21) He has amazing things in store as you live as His girl! ≪

STUDY GUIDE

What was one thing that was especially helpful to you in this chapter?

_____

_____

What is one step that you will take today to apply it to your own life?

_____

_____

What is one struggle that you face in this area that you can ask Jesus to help you overcome?

_____

_____

Look up these Bible verses and write what Jesus shows you:

- Philippians 1:21

_____

_____

- Galatians 2:20

_____

_____

- 2 Corinthians 5:14-15

_____

_____

_____

_____

Pray or write out a prayer of response to Jesus.

_____

_____

_____

_____

Write the Focus Statement for this chapter.

_____

_____

_____

_____

You can write any additional thoughts here.

_____

_____

_____

HE WORKS

THROUGH

HIS GIRL

*to impact
the world*

CHAPTER 8

Serving and Sharing Jesus

SERVING THE ONE WHO HAS CHANGED YOUR LIFE AND SHARING HIM WITH A WORLD THAT NEEDS HIM

"…We cannot but speak of what we have seen and heard."
(Acts 4:20)

What — or who — has changed your life?
You know the answer – Jesus! Listen to this:

> When you come to Jesus, and He has changed – and is changing – your life, your natural outflow is to want to serve Him and for others to know Him, too. As you do, as He works through you, you experience Him in new ways, have the joy of watching Him work, and see others' lives be transformed by His life through you, in a way that lasts forever!

If you found the cure to a disease, you would want to share it with the world, wouldn't you? Get this – you have the answer to the deepest need of people's souls and their eternal salvation – Jesus! You want to serve and share the One you know and love! Do you see this? As His, you have the call, and privilege, to serve and share about the One Who has changed your life – as He works through you. It is the outflow of your relationship with Jesus. The more you know Jesus and how He has changed your life, the more you will want to share Him with others. You will want people to know the Jesus you love! You will say with the disciples, *"…we cannot but speak of what we have seen and heard."* (Acts 4:20)

Why it Is So Important and What it Is

Think of those in your world. Just like you were, they are eternal souls, headed for hell, and desperately in need of Jesus! Or, they are like you are – they are His and are longing for encouragement in Jesus. The Lord has chosen to use you to share Jesus with the world. What a big privilege!

He has called you to serve and share Him!

You have the call and privilege, to serve and share about the One Who has changed your life — as He works through you.

Serving – This is doing all you do for Jesus, serving Him wherever He places you, seeing life as ministry, discovering ways to serve, understanding different ways to serve in different seasons, and serving Him by serving people for His sake and glory!

Sharing the Gospel and Jesus – This is the privilege of sharing the Good News of Jesus and the salvation He offers, your personal testimony, how good Jesus is, and discipleship with others!

We have the joy of looking at both of these in this chapter! Aren't these both incredible?

As Jesus physically left this world and returned to Heaven leaving His Holy Spirit in those who are His, He gave this to you as His girl as His final call:

> *"And Jesus came and said to them, 'All authority in heaven and on earth has been given to me. Go therefore and make disciples of all nations, baptizing them in the name of the Father and of the Son and of the Holy Spirit, teaching them to observe all that I have commanded you. And behold, I am with you always, to the end of the age.'"* (Matthew 28:18-20)

As His girl, you have been entrusted with this call – it is a call for everyone who is Christ's!

You have the privilege to be a part of the beautiful work He is doing. This is so powerful. You get to serve Jesus and share the Gospel and Jesus with people. He works in their hearts by the Holy Spirit to save souls, grow disciples, and build His Kingdom. That is so remarkable, isn't it?

How It Changes Your Life

Friend, listen to this – while He is impacting others through you, this is transforming to you in your own walk and life with Him!

Here are three ways you are impacted as you share Jesus:

- ⋙ There is no greater joy, next to experiencing Jesus for yourself, than watching Him transform someone else's life.
- ⋙ Sharing Jesus only confirms and deepens in your own heart the beautiful realities you know about Him.
- ⋙ You experience Him in new ways, and your faith grows as He works through you.

When I personally came to know and experience Jesus, I was so fulfilled. My heart responded, "This is what I have been searching for! I want people to know You like this! I will go anywhere, and do anything, Jesus!" He led me step-by-step in ways to serve and share Him. Through serving and sharing, it has been an amazing journey of knowing Him more. As He has given me opportunities to serve and share Him, He has deepened my own walk with Him! It is so wonderful!

His Role and Yours

It is so important – and powerful – to understand the difference between Jesus' role and yours.

Let's look at the difference between the roles:

Your role: to be an instrument for Him to work through, place your faith in Him, rely on His strength, share Jesus, give what you have received, shine His light, and trust Him for the fruit.

Think of a pitcher that holds water – it is a container for something that gives life. It is filled and worked through, right? That is what your call and role is – to be an available tool in His hands to meet the spiritual needs of those who are thirsty for Him! I love this amazing verse, *"…We have this treasure in jars of clay, to show that the surpassing power belongs to God and not to us."* (2 Corinthians 4:7)

It is when Jesus is flowing through you to touch others for Himself that lives can be impacted for eternity!

His role: to lead you, provide opportunities for you, empower you, work through you, and do His transforming work in people's hearts and lives.

Jesus is the only One Who can work and transform hearts in a way that will last forever!

Listen to this incredible verse: *"Not that we are sufficient in ourselves to claim anything as coming from us, but our sufficiency is*

from God…" (2 Corinthians 3:5)

This is so beautiful and freeing, isn't it? The magnificent thing is that in this way, He gets the glory, you get the joy of being used, and people are blessed as a result!

The Power of Prayer

Prayer is powerful because it is only when God moves that hearts are changed forever! Pray for the Lord to work through you, and in the hearts of those you share with, for people to be saved and encouraged in Him, and for Him to send more people out to share Him! *"…The harvest is plentiful, but the laborers are few; therefore pray earnestly to the Lord of the harvest to send out laborers into his harvest."* (Matthew 9:37-38) He loves to answer these prayers in His perfect way and time.

> *As His girl, the question is not "if" you are in ministry — you are. The question is, "Where is Jesus calling me to serve and share Him right now?"*

Life as a Ministry

Life is a mission field. Your life can be a ministry, and every moment is an opportunity to shine, serve, or share Jesus wherever you are. You can be open at any moment, wherever you are, to what Jesus wants to do through you. It can include: loving the person in front of you, speaking a word of encouragement about Jesus (For example, "I see Jesus in your life through your servant heart." Or, "Right now, Jesus is showing me how much He loves us."), sharing the Gospel with someone you cross paths with, and so much more.

As His girl, the question is not "if" you are in ministry or are a missionary – you are. The question is just, "Where is Jesus calling me to serve and share Him right now?"

Shining Jesus from Your Life

You got a glimpse of this in the *Growing in Jesus* chapter. Jesus is filling you and shining from you! Let Jesus shine from you wherever you are! People see Jesus real in you – the genuine evidence of Jesus in your life. They see His light in your eyes, love radiating through you, and likeness in your actions. Their response might be, "I want what she has!"

So many people will never go to church, but they will cross paths with you. They will see something different – Jesus in you. This might open the chance to share Him – whether to speak His name, share the Gospel with them, give them a Gospel tract, invite them to church, share His goodness in your life, etc. And others, who are His, and who cross paths with you, will be encouraged in Jesus! *"You are the light of the world... let your light shine before others, so that they may see your good works and give glory to your Father who is in heaven."* (Matthew 5:14, 16)

Practical Ideas of Ways to Serve & Share Jesus

This list of ideas is just a starting point of what you can do now to serve and share Jesus right where you are. The ideas are endless! If your focus is serving Jesus and sharing Jesus and the Gospel, there is no end to the creative ways to reach out to others for His glory. As you keep seeking Him and allowing Him to use you, He will show you more and more opportunities to serve and share Him in every situation of life!

- Serve your family (helping with cooking, caring for siblings, dishes, cleaning, laundry)
- Teach your siblings Bible verses, do a Bible study with them, pray together

⋙ Serve as a family – seek to have a family ministry (show hospitality, volunteer, share Christ)

⋙ Write notes, send e-mails, or make calls of encouragement in the Lord to others (your friends, younger girls or children, pastor, missionaries, parents)

⋙ Pray for family, people's salvation, missionaries, friends, etc.

⋙ Pass out Gospel tracts

⋙ Write a tract, record your testimony

⋙ Share the Gospel

⋙ Be involved in ministry at church, when you are able. Help with Sunday School, children's ministries, in the kitchen, in the nursery, etc.

⋙ Earn and find ways to save money so that you can support missions or sponsor a child in need whom you can tell about Jesus

⋙ Mentor those younger than you

⋙ Start a discipleship group for girls

⋙ Host a Bible study with your friends and those in your life you want to reach for Christ

⋙ Write an article, magazine, or book that will encourage other girls in their walk with God

⋙ Verbally encourage someone for their character, Christ-likeness, etc.

⋙ Sing hymns or play an instrument at a nursing home

⋙ Help a widow – grocery shop, fix things around her house, work in her yard

⋙ Make a meal for a mom who just had a baby

⋙ Share what the Lord has been teaching you, tell what He did in answer to prayer, talk about Jesus and how good He is, share what you are reading in the Bible, etc.

⫸ Seek to be of help when you are at other people's homes or at events

⫸ Do all that you do for the Lord and His glory – "...*Do all to the glory of God.*" (1 Corinthians 10:31)

There is so much that you can do right where you are! You don't have to wait to be a missionary in another country. It starts right where the Lord has placed you right now. Seek the Lord and look for how you can serve and share Him today. Don't underestimate what God can and will do through you if you are willing!

What is one way that you can serve or share Jesus today?

_____

_____

_____

Remember that there is no small way to serve or share Jesus — it all matters!

So picture yourself doing that thing that you just wrote down. For example, say you feel the Lord leading you to reach out to a younger girl at church and encourage her in Jesus. You could make the effort to talk with her at church and get to know her. Then you could write her a note of encouragement during the week and share a Bible verse with her that has been encouraging to you. When you see her again, you could talk with her and see if there is any way you could pray for her. You can nurture the relationship for as long as the Lord has planned. Do you get the idea? I encourage you to find one step to take towards that thing today! Remember that there is no small way to serve or share Jesus – it all matters!

Sharing the Gospel and Jesus

How to Share the Gospel: You only need to know how you were saved to tell someone else how to be saved. Remember, it is the Holy Spirit's work to save them and your job to share Him! It is helpful to have key parts of the Gospel in mind to share with others.

A Basic Overview of the Gospel

To remember the treasure of the Gospel to you and to be ready to share it with others, it is helpful to periodically think through the basic truths of the Gospel, which include:

You were created to walk with and glorify God – *"…Whom I created for my glory, whom I formed and made."* (Isaiah 43:7)

There is the problem of sin that separates you from God – *"…For all have sinned and fall short of the glory of God…"* (Romans 3:23)

God provided a solution to your sin in Jesus – *"For God so loved the world, that he gave his only Son, that whoever believes in him should not perish but have eternal life."* (John 3:16)

To be saved, you must personally respond and place your faith in Jesus as your Lord and Savior and follow Him – *"…If you confess with your mouth that Jesus is Lord and believe in your heart that God raised him from the dead, you will be saved."* (Romans 10:9)

You can refer back to the Gospel section of the *Becoming His Girl* chapter for more details that you can use as you share the Gospel.

You can share the Gospel and your personal testimony with them and then ask them if they would like to trust in and follow Jesus as their Savior and Lord personally. It is so important to have this ready at any time to share the best News ever! It is the most essential News in all of life! You can copy these key points and put them in your purse or backpack to have until you memorize them by heart. The main thing is to share it! The Lord can use even your weakest attempts. Do not be discouraged if they do not respond.

You might be sowing a seed of Truth in their heart that the Lord will use to bring fruit later! You are like a messenger, who has been entrusted with an important message – you are not the message, but the carrier of it. Sharing the Gospel is your call, and the results are His. (You must share Jesus, and they must be saved, before they can be discipled in Jesus.) This is the best news you could ever share with anyone!

Listen to these beautiful and motivating verses: *"How then will they call on him in whom they have not believed? And how are they to believe in him of whom they have never heard? And how are they to hear without someone preaching? And how are they to preach unless they are sent? As it is written, 'How beautiful are the feet of those who preach the good news!'"* (Romans 10:14-15)

Sharing Your Testimony

Picture yourself asking someone, "Can I tell you what changed my life?"

It is so powerful to recognize, know, and share your personal testimony of how Jesus saved you and how He has transformed your life! I love to call it your "Jesus Story." You can think it through and write it out for your own encouragement and to be able to share it with others!

Some helpful points to include in your testimony are:

>> The need in your life before Jesus
>> How you came to Jesus
>> How He changed – and continues to change – your life

It can be short and simple.

For example, a basic version is: "I was separated from God by my sin. Then I heard about Jesus and that He had died to take the punishment for my sin. I trusted Him as my Savior and Lord. He saved me. He has changed my life and will continue to work until I go to be with Him in Heaven someday!"

You can write your personalized version of your testimony here.

How I was before Jesus:

_____

_____

_____

_____

_____

How I came to Jesus:

_____

_____

_____

_____

How He changed – and continues to change – my life:

_____

_____

_____

_____

Now, you can review this and have it ready to share at any time with those who do not know about Jesus! And also as an encouragement to those who do know Him.

You can also share testimonies of what Jesus is doing in your life now – in knowing Him more, His transforming your heart, and His work in your life. This is an encouragement to those who are His and a witness to those who are not.

Your testimony is so powerful! No one can deny what Jesus has done in your life! And you can tell them, "He can do it in your life, too!" Again, it is like the disciples said in the Bible, *"…we cannot but speak of what we have seen and heard."* (Acts 4:20)

A Reality as You Share

This is a powerful truth to cling to as you share the Gospel and your testimony of Jesus' work in your life: *"'…You are my witnesses,' declares the LORD, 'and I am God.'"* (Isaiah 43:12) Do you see the power of this? You are a witness – sharing what you know, experienced, and have seen of Jesus. He is God – He is the One Who works in hearts by His Spirit and can bring results! The sharing is yours and the results are His!

Serving Jesus: A General and Special Way to Serve Jesus

When you look in the Bible, you see that all Christians are called to serve and share Jesus. There are general ways in which we are all called to do this. Then there are areas where God gives gifts and calls each person to serve in specific ways that stem from those general ways.

So, for example, we are all called to serve Jesus – that is a general call. Then, from that general call, He might give one person a call to serve Jesus through going on the mission field, another person might help in Sunday School, and another might invite a friend to church. These are all unique ways to fulfill the call. They are just fulfilled differently! Do you see how this works?

The Lord gives us the powerful example of the church being the Body of Christ and having many members — like the human body has eyes, ears, feet, a mouth, etc., and all are important! Romans 12:4-6 says, *"For as in one body we have many members, and the members do not all have the same function, so we, though many, are one body in Christ, and individually members one of another. Having gifts that differ according to the grace given to us, let us use them."* As everyone works together and uses each of their gifts for His glory, He does amazing things.

Be faithful in what Jesus has called you to do right now.

You have the joy of answering His general call and of serving Him in the special ways He calls you to serve!

Be Faithful Wherever Jesus Places You

He has you right where you are, right now, for a reason!

"For we are his workmanship, created in Christ Jesus for good works, which God prepared beforehand, that we should walk in them." (Ephesians 2:10)

Think of someone who Jesus used to impact your life for Him. How did He work through them? He wants to work through you to impact others for Himself, too! Listen to Jesus. Be faithful in what Jesus has called you to do right now. And He will use that as a ripple effect, and as your part in His grand work, His biggest story of redemption, and building His Kingdom!

When I had just begun my first discipleship group for girls in my house, I loved it so much, and I knew I was called to do it. I was walking into the laundry room, and talking to Jesus, "Lord, I know that You have called me to disciple girls and I love it so much. But, what is my place in reaching the people in China who have never heard of You?" It was as if He brought back to mind that at the first meeting, I had done an ice breaker activity with the girls. I had asked them each to write what was the greatest desire of their hearts, besides knowing Jesus. Two of them said it was to be a missionary. It was as if the Lord was showing me that if I was faithful where He placed me, He would work through me to impact the girls for Him. Then as He works through them to impact others for Himself, I would have a part in that. Isn't He amazing?

The main thing to keep your eyes on is your own walk with Jesus, love for Him, heart to share Him, and openness to how He would have you do these things right now. He will lead you in exciting ways!

And remember this – your call to serve and share Him remains the same for your whole life, but how He calls you to live that out may look different in the changing seasons of life. Another way we could say this is – your ways to minister, and your mission fields, can change over time and seasons, but the mission is still the same.

One season might have you mentoring a group of younger girls. Another season might have you raising your kids for Jesus and reaching out to the people you cross paths with in your daily life. Another season might have you sick in bed praying for, and writing notes of encouragement to missionaries.

What This Can Look Like in Your Life

What can this look like in your life? Stop and think about that for a moment. You could raise money for missionaries, reach out to a lonely girl, and share about Jesus with her, help in the nursery at church, mentor a younger girl and so much more! What is Jesus

putting on your heart? He can give you special burdens for a par-
ticular age group, need, country, etc., or for people in general.

I have been so blessed as I have seen girls who wrote encouraging notes to others, helped their families with foster care, served in
the nursery at church, started a discipleship group to mentor girls
in Jesus, and so much more. In my own
life, what it has looked like has included: praying with someone, giving Gospel tracts to cashiers at the store, making someone a meal to support them in
serving Jesus, mentoring girls in Jesus,
going on missions trips, writing about
Jesus, etc. There are so many ways to
serve and share Jesus! Jesus has amazing ways for you to serve and share Him
as you look to Him, and just start somewhere!

Sharing and serving Him should be the outflow of your relationship with Jesus!

What is one way you will receive His grace to share or serve Him
today?

To Remember as You Serve and Share

It is important to remember to keep the right perspective as you
serve and share. Like trying to walk with cloudy glasses, having the
wrong perspective can lead to struggles. But having the right perspective, by His grace, can lead you to joy, power, and fruitfulness
in serving and sharing Jesus. More than anything, your relationship
with Jesus should always be first! He wants your heart more than
your hands. Sharing and serving Him should be the outflow of your
relationship with Jesus!

It is so important to remember, and to serve and share, from
these truths:

⇒ Who He is

⇒ Who you are in Him

⇒ It is by His power in you

⇒ It is a call to answer

⇒ Your call is to share – His job is the results

Remember that your true identity and value to God come from who you are in Jesus because you are His, not from what He does through you. This is very important. You do not serve and share Jesus to earn or keep your salvation or God's favor. You serve as an overflow of your salvation and His favor that He has given to you in Christ!

You are, and will remain, who you are in Jesus, no matter what. Then that identity in Him gives you a call. You serve and share Jesus from that place. *"For by grace you have been saved through faith. And this is not your own doing; it is the gift of God, not a result of works, so that no one may boast. For we are his workmanship, created in Christ Jesus for good works, which God prepared beforehand, that we should walk in them."* (Ephesians 2:8-10)

Always keep in mind that it is all about Jesus and His glory – building His Kingdom and family! This results in His glory, your joy, and the blessing of others. *"…Let your light shine before others, so that they may see your good works and give glory to your Father who is in heaven."* (Matthew 5:16)

He Uses the Weak

Are you ready for some good news? He uses the weak. He does not expect you to become all polished before He uses you. As you follow Jesus' call, He will make you into what you need to be for what He has called you to do. Listen to Matthew 4:19, where Jesus said, *"...Follow me, and I will make you fishers of men."* He equips you for what He has called you to do as you follow Him.

Struggles That Can Hold You Back

So, let's be honest – this can sometimes be scary, right? While this is so exciting, and you know it is what you are called to do, things can sneak in that hold you back and stop you from fulfilling this amazing mission! Let's look at some struggles together.

Here are some common struggles:

- fear of what people will think, say, or do in response
- fear of what people will think, say, or do in response
  fear of doing it wrong
- fear of the results
- feeling not equipped or ready
- insecurity
- laziness
- selfishness
- being distracted or feeling dull
- having the wrong motive – doing it for glory from or fear of people
- making it about you and your image, instead of Jesus and His Kingdom
- …and more!

Is there one, or more, of these that you especially face?

_____

_____

_____

It is a reality that you will likely face many of them, but the greater reality is that Jesus, and what He has equipped you with in Him, can overpower those things! Always remember this – *"...He who is in you is greater than he who is in the world."* (1 John 4:4) The enemy – the devil – will try to stop you. He fears what will happen if Jesus uses you to impact the world for Himself. Remember the truth, who you are in Jesus, and most of all, Who He is! Ask Jesus for His help to overcome each struggle. Let the value of sharing Him be greater than any fear or struggle!

I have had times where I felt the call to do something, and I was scared! For example, there was a time where the Lord had laid on my heart a testimony of something that He had done in my life to share with a group. I was so scared to do it! But I knew He wanted me to, and I got up to share. I was shaking all over – even my cheeks were wiggling! I shared the testimony.

You have the joy and privilege of sharing the One Who has changed your life — and Who can change people's lives!

When I sat down, I felt so much joy and knew I had done what the Lord wanted – even if the whole room thought I was silly. This led to so many opportunities, in His call for me, to share Him through speaking. He is so amazing! It is being surrendered to Jesus and caring more about what He thinks than what people think.

There will be times when you miss opportunities – or shrink back in fear. I know I have. These are times to ask Jesus for forgiveness and help to follow His call in the future. Jesus lives through you to impact others for Himself.

You share and leave the results up to Him. Whether they respond or not, you have done what you are called to do, and Jesus is pleased by your heart and obedience. If they respond, it is such a joy! If you are made fun of, rejected, or persecuted, here is a verse for you: *"Blessed are those who are persecuted for righteousness' sake, for theirs is the kingdom of heaven. Blessed are you when others revile you and persecute you and utter all kinds of evil against you falsely on my account. Rejoice and be glad, for your reward is great in heaven…"* (Matthew 5:10-12)

Remember, every person is an eternal soul, either headed for hell without Jesus, or one of His, who needs encouragement in Him! This will really help to motivate you! Again, it is like telling someone the cure for a disease. You know they desperately need the cure, it is something that you have been entrusted with, and that you are called to share it! Do not let anything stop you!

A Beautiful Reality

Jesus said, *"I say to you, as you did it to one of the least of these my brothers, you did it to me."* (Matthew 25:40) What you do to others in serving them, it is as if you are doing it to Jesus. It brings you joy to serve the One you love!

Serving and Sharing Your Jesus

So, friend, Jesus has changed your life. You have the joy of – and call to – serve and share Him. His Spirit within you will empower you to do it. You know Jesus more and see His glory as you serve and share Him! He will bring eternal fruit for His glory! You have this one life to share Jesus – and can do that until your last breath.

Let's picture this in your daily life – you are going about your day today, with your eyes open to how Jesus wants to work through you. Then, He opens an opportunity, and you take it! For example, He opens a door in conversation to share the Gospel with a neighbor, gives you a chance to pray with a friend, shows you your mom's need for help with dinner, etc. Be open and ready to Jesus using you to reach anyone and anywhere He leads you! This is your call and privilege!

Isn't that extraordinary? Know that whatever you have done for Jesus is seen by Him and will bring joy to His heart – no matter the results!

Application Step

What is one thing that you can do today to serve or share Jesus?

_____

_____

_____

Call To Action

Let's listen to Jesus' call again:

> *"And Jesus came and said to them, 'All authority in heaven and on earth has been given to me. Go therefore and make disciples of all nations, baptizing them in the name of the Father and of the Son and of the Holy Spirit, teaching them to observe all that I have commanded you. And behold, I am with you always, to the end of the age.'"* (Matthew 28:18-20)

We see in these verses:

- Why you can go – "*...All authority in heaven and on earth has been given to me...*" (Matthew 28:18)
- A call to go – "*Go... into all the world, and preach the Gospel to every creature...*" (Matthew 28:19)
- A promise and what empowers you to go – "*...I am with you always...*" (Matthew 28:20)

This is your call! Your response can be, "*...Here I am! Send me.*" (Isaiah 6:8) You can pray something like this: "Dear Jesus, please help me to shine and share You to the world around me! I trust You to work through me and in their hearts!"

You have the joy and privilege of sharing the One Who has changed your life – and Who can change people's lives! All that will last forever are Jesus and your relationship with Him, His Word, and people's souls. He is in you, has changed you, has given you a message to share, and will work through you to reach the world for His glory!

Go serve and share the One Who has changed your life, and watch Him change others, too! ≪

STUDY GUIDE

What was one thing that was especially helpful to you in this chapter?

_____

_____

_____

What is one step that you will take today to apply it to your own life?

_____

_____

What is one struggle that you face in this area that you can ask Jesus to help you overcome?

_____

_____

Look up these Bible verses and write what Jesus shows you:

- Acts 4:20

_____

_____

- 2 Corinthians 4:7

_____

_____

_____

- Matthew 28:18-20

_____

_____

_____

_____

Pray or write out a prayer of response to Jesus.

_____

_____

_____

_____

Write the Focus Statement for this chapter.

_____

_____

_____

You can write any additional thoughts here.

_____

_____

_____

Jesus is writing

A STORY

FOR HIS GLORY

in your life

CHAPTER 9

Your Jesus Story

YOUR UNIQUE LIFE STORY FOR HIS GLORY AS YOU FOLLOW JESUS

"…Follow me." (Luke 5:27)

....

What is your story?

Once upon a time, there was a girl – and she was you. Jesus is writing a beautiful story in your life. Soak in this reality:

> The Lord is writing the great story of redemption for His glory in all of history as He draws people to Himself. You are part of that story – and when you become His girl, you begin your Jesus story for His glory. He is writing a special and unique story in your own life that will glorify Him and fit into His great story! As you follow Jesus in surrender – empowered by His life in you, He unfolds the amazing story that He has for your life – for His greatest glory, your deepest good, and the biggest blessing of others – as a part of His eternal story.

It is a story that unfolds until you see Him face to face! It is so spectacular! Are you ready to take a look?

What This Story Is and Why It Matters

So, why does this story matter? Stop, ask yourself, and answer this question – why were you created? For His glory, right? So, you were created for this story because you were created for His glory. *"...Created for my glory..."* (Isaiah 43:7) The grand story He is writing and your story within that story are all about Him. *"...To live is Christ..."* (Philippians 1:21) You have the privilege of being part of that grand story – a story for His glory!

Here is a beautiful thing about His ways – He always works things in this story for His greatest glory, your deepest good, and the most blessing for others. They always go hand in hand. Isn't that incredible?

Do you love a good story? This is the amazing thing – your Jesus story is your personal story with your Jesus, lived in a step-by-step journey with Him as He unfolds His perfect plan for you. You see, you are called to follow in a personal relationship with Him – and as you do, He leads you into His plan for you. You were meant for this personal relationship. He did not just create you, save you, give you a plan, and tell you to go live out that plan on your own. You were meant to walk it with Him. In this moment, He is right there with you – He is in you, with you, and empowers you to live in this story by His Spirit in you. Take a second to pause and let that soak into your mind and heart. Whatever you face in your story, He is with you. You are walking with your Savior and your best Friend. You have all you need. Isn't that the best? *"You make known to me the path of life; in your presence there is fullness of joy; at your right hand are pleasures forevermore."* (Psalm 16:11)

Jesus is your story. That is what your Jesus story is — your testimony of how Jesus saved you, who He has been to you, how He has transformed you, what He has done in your life, and what He will continue to do until you see Him face to face. Your life story is meant to, and can, point to Him and lift Him up — showcasing the realness and goodness of your Jesus!

This is a real story, and you are a real part of it! Like we said before, it is not a fairytale — it is a real-life adventure with Jesus. It is so exciting! You have an incredible purpose, and He has a unique plan for you. It is the greatest adventure you could have! It is your own Jesus story. Don't you want to live it?

Your Jesus story is your personal story with your Jesus, lived in a step-by-step journey with Him as He unfolds His perfect plan for you.

You Can Live It

When I came to Jesus and knew and trusted His heart, I knew that I could trust my all to Him. He would only do what is truly best for me. As He called me to follow Him in surrender, He has written a story beyond what I would have imagined. He will do this for you, too!

I have loved watching girls follow Him in surrender and seeing His individual stories for them unfold. You can trust your life into the hands of the One Who gave His life for you. Will you trust Him? He will write a story for His glory in your own life! *"…What no eye has seen, nor ear heard, nor the heart of man imagined, what God has prepared for those who love him…"* (1 Corinthians 2:9)

Realities About His Story for You

Like peeking to glimpse pieces of an adventure story, there are some absolutely amazing realities about His story for you that will thrill you!

Let's first review some realities we have already looked at in previous chapters and this chapter. This story: is about Jesus, it is for His glory, is with Jesus, has every step empowered by His Spirit in you, is founded on and lived in the Truth of His Word, impacts eternity by Jesus living and working through you, and ends with Heaven is your home. Do you remember these?

Now, let's look at some other incredible realities:

He has a perfect plan for you. Jeremiah 29:11 says, *"For I know the plans I have for you, declares the LORD, plans for welfare and not for evil, to give you a future and a hope."* He has a perfect plan. You can trust Him. This is so beautiful – it is a plan of His heart. *"The counsel of the Lord stands forever, the plans of His heart to all generations."* (Psalm 33:11) You know Him and know that you can trust His heart, even when you cannot see all of His plan or what He is doing!

His plan is for His glory, your good, and the blessing of others. As we looked at above, the beautiful thing about His ways is that He always works things in this story for His greatest glory, your deepest good, and the most blessing for others. They always go hand in hand. This makes His plan for you so exciting – and purposeful!

You are unique. Hear this: God made you individually and intentionally, with a special plan for your life. *"I praise you, for I am fearfully and wonderfully made. Wonderful are your works; my soul knows it very well."* (Psalm 139:14) He made you on purpose and for a purpose. He has created you uniquely and beautifully – with special gifts, personality, features, etc. He is pleased with how He made you uniquely – even the things you see as a weakness or would like to change about yourself! You are perfectly formed and made by God. Live as the person He made you to be – in line with His Word and Spirit – and you will display His glory in a unique way!

Your story is unique to you. It is so wonderful! Your story is so unique, and you have your own journey with Jesus. The general call for all who are His is the same – to know and glorify Him. But the way that each person lives it out looks different. He knows how you can best do that as part of the big story. He will write your unique story to accomplish that end. Doesn't it make your story with Jesus so personal? *"…In your book were written, every one of them, the days that were formed for me, when as yet there was none of them."* (Psalm 139:16) Isn't that beautiful?

It is your adventure with Jesus. This story with Jesus is the greatest adventure you could live. You were made for this. Jesus is with you through every step of life, so you have all you need. Endless possibilities of what He has in store await you. It is a personal relationship journey you walk with Jesus. The adventure will unfold, as you take each step with Him. You live this story hand-in-hand with Jesus. *"For I, the LORD your God, hold your right hand; it is I who say to you, 'Fear not, I am the one who helps you.'"* (Isaiah 41:13) It is an epic adventure – with Jesus, by Jesus, and for Jesus. It is better than any adventure book! You are personally living the greatest adventure!

He works in it all to increasingly help you know, grow, follow, and overflow Him more. He works in all of life to accomplish this – through the trials, joys, and questions. *"And we know that for those who love God all things work together for good, for those who are called according to his purpose."* (Romans 8:28) We will look at this more below.

You are right here, right now, for a purpose. Jesus has had His girls in every generation – who were His, knew Him, loved Him, and lived to make Him known. And in this generation, He has called you! He could have had you born at any time in history, but He has chosen to have you live here right now to know Him, to be a part of what He is doing, and be a light to this generation! *"…And who* *knows whether you have not come to the kingdom for such a time as this?"* (Esther 4:14)

You know how the story ends. Isn't that wonderful? There is such an amazing peace when you know that – no matter what you face in life between now and then – Jesus is working His story in your life! Heaven is your home, and Jesus is victorious over all. The story that Jesus is writing will always end in victory! Isn't that beautiful, and doesn't it fill your heart with comfort? You will see your Jesus face to face, be with Him, and worship Him forever!

Aren't these truths beautiful, exciting, and thrilling? They will be a reality for your life!

Is there one of these realities that especially means a lot to you right now?

Following Jesus in Surrender

Friend, as His girl, you are a follower of Jesus. This is your call and joy! There is no one else you would rather follow. You know His heart, and His plans for you are perfect. Jesus' call is *"…Follow me."* (Luke 5:27) As you do, He will walk with you, work in you, lead you into all He has for you, and be glorified through your life. This is what you are called to for your life!

Following Jesus in surrender is to say from your heart, "I am Yours, Jesus! Do anything You want, Jesus. I will follow You." and then seek to grow in living like it! At the time of your salvation, you give your life to Jesus and are forever His. You then grow in living in and from that surrender every moment of your life. It is you moment-by-moment giving Him the pen to write the story of your life.

When you try to write your own story, it is like a toddler grabbing the pen from a famous author – and scribbling. He writes masterpieces. Again, Matthew 16:24-25 shows you the beautiful truth that Jesus said, *"'…If anyone would come after me, let him deny himself and take up his cross and follow me. For whoever would save his life will lose it, but whoever loses his life for my sake will find it.'"*

You are a follower of Jesus.

Surrender is giving your all to the One Who gave His all for you. Bring all of your hopes, dreams, and plans and lay them in surrender at His feet. It is like Jesus is asking you to lay down the dirt that you are clutching in your hands so that He can give you the treasure of Himself and His plan. He knows how to write the perfect story, and He sees the big picture. Someday you will see the perfection of His plan.

For now, it is looking to Him in faith and following Him in obedience – embracing Jesus and whatever His story holds for you at this moment! For now, you only get a glimpse of His plan and trust it in faith. But, in Heaven, you will see and stand in awe of His perfect plan! Open your hands in surrender and watch Him do what only He can do. You will see the story unfold and be amazed at His wisdom. He is the One *"…who is able to do far more abundantly than all we ask or think…"* (Ephesians 3:20)

What This Looks Like in Your Life — and the Personal Results

It is like stepping into the pages of a storybook as you personally follow Jesus wherever He leads. You will experience Him and the journey you are created to walk with Him – and watch the story unfold for yourself! You live this story out step by step, moment by moment, as you walk with Him, and He lives in and through you. Every day is a fresh part of the adventure. You can wake up in the morning saying, "Jesus, You are with me, You are for me, and You have a plan for Your glory, my good, and the blessing of others today."

As you live following Jesus, surrendering moment-by-moment, walking in fellowship with Him, listening to His Word, and living in obedience to what He calls you to do, you will see Him do amazing things in your life and story. I am so excited for you! It is so thrilling what Jesus will do with a life that says, "Anything, Jesus!" As you give Him the pen to write the story of your life, He will write a masterpiece beyond anything you could imagine. He will lead you to His best, where He will be lifted up, you will experience joy, and others will be impacted as Jesus lives in and through you. They will see the reality of Jesus in your life and be touched by Him.

Walk in the real light of Jesus, the Holy Spirit in you, the Gospel, and the realities that are yours as His girl.

As you live surrendered to Jesus, your own unique story unfolds in your life that lifts Him up in a special way! Just like there are many chapters in a story, there will be both times of joy that you can hardly believe are real when you see Him work, and also hard times where you do not understand what He is doing (we will look at this more). In both situations, you can know that He is fulfilling His purposes for His glory and your good. He is glorified in your life as you say, "Jesus is better than anything!" in all of your circumstances. When I surrendered my life to follow Jesus, I had no idea what the journey He would take me on would be like. I would not trade my journey with Jesus for the world.

Can you imagine what daily surrender to Jesus will look like in your life? Stop and think about that for a moment. You get up in the morning, affirm your surrender of yourself and day to Jesus afresh, take the next step with your eyes on Jesus and say, "What next, Jesus?". You then follow what He shows you. This can include choices of what you do, where you go, how you spend your time, where you give money, dreams for the future – and so much more.

Walk in and live out your story in the real light of Jesus, the Holy Spirit in you, the Gospel, and the realities that are yours as His girl. This may look like yielding to Jesus the desire to spend time on your own interests in order to serve others, or yielding your dreams of marriage and trusting Jesus for your future, and so much more.

You surrender your life, trusting Him to give and do what is best! Or, maybe it is following Him as He leads you to reach out to a person He puts on your heart, or filling your soul with more of His Word and watching the beauty of what He does as a result. As you take steps of practical surrender in your own life, you will see Him bring your story more to life!

You can fill this in:

> I can surrender to Jesus in _____
> and follow Him by _____
> _____.

When you do, you will see Him work! As you follow Him in surrender, you will see Him work in areas of your story, such as in your relationship with Him, interaction with others, how you live your days, choices you make, questions for your future, areas you seek growth, and so much more. He has amazing things in store as you embrace Him and every moment of your story with Him – knowing He has incredible purposes in it. Experience it for yourself, and you will see that nothing compares. It is the life you were made for and do not want to miss! Follow Him, friend. *"The Lord will fulfill his purpose for me..."* (Psalm 138:8)

There is an Incredible Purpose in the Whole Story

This makes me so excited! In every moment of your story, Jesus is working to fulfill His purpose – to help you know Him more, become more like Him, and shine His goodness more! Isn't that incredible? In every season and chapter of your story, the reality of walking with Him, growing in Him, and sharing Him never changes. The heart purpose is the same – it just looks different in different seasons and chapters of life.

He has you, at this moment, where you can best know, grow in, follow, and glorify Him!

I have seen this in my own life. For me, in one season, it was being faithful in schoolwork. In another, it was following Him to start a ministry for girls. In another, it was trying to heal from a long-term illness. In another, it was getting married and moving to a new place – and the journey continues! With every day and season, every line and chapter of your story, He is fulfilling His purposes in your life.

And grasp this – He has you, at this moment, where you can best know, grow in, follow, and glorify Him right now! Doesn't that add so much meaning and purpose to where you are today? Today, He could have you at home doing the dishes, teaching Sunday School in another country, sick in bed, or so many other things.

The goal is to follow and be with Jesus, wherever He wants you to be. For your heart to say, "I just want to be with You, Jesus." As you walk with Him as His girl right where He has you, He is going to do phenomenal things as He writes this story for His glory in your life! *"I will instruct you and teach you in the way you should go; I will counsel you with my eye upon you."* (Psalm 32:8) Exciting, isn't it?

Where does Jesus have you right now where you can do this?

_____

_____

_____

How to Embrace Your Story for His Glory

So, how can you embrace this story? There are so many ways to embrace your story for His glory. Let's look at some wonderful ways together!

Daily fix and keep your eyes on Jesus. You can open your eyes in the morning and pray, "Jesus, I love You, I am Yours, do all that You want in and through me today. I want You and need You. I will seek to follow You by Your help!" *"Let me hear in the morning of your steadfast love, for in you I trust. Make me know the way I should go, for to you I lift up my soul."* (Psalm 143:8) As you walk with your eyes on Him, He can guide you through the day!

Stay close to Jesus and share life with Him. You can say, "Jesus, I want to be with You – wherever You are leading me. If You are there, that is all I need." It is so sweet walking with Him all throughout the day and asking, "Jesus, what do You want to show me of Yourself right now? How do You want to grow me right now? What do You want to teach me right now? What do You want to do through me right now?" With your eyes on Him, your heart in fellowship with Him, you seeking His guidance, and then following

His leading throughout the day, you will walk more and more in the story He has for you as He guides and empowers your steps.

Keep the vision of Who He is and what He has called you to in front of you. Most of all, it is important to have Jesus as your vision — and then to let Him remind you from His Word, and to personally show you the vision He has for your life, as He guides you by the Holy Spirit. It can be so helpful to remind yourself of your vision daily to set your course for the day!

It can also be helpful to write it out, keep it in front of you, and review that vision statement. For example, you could write out and place somewhere you will see it to remind yourself: "My purpose is to know, follow, and glorify Jesus." As you take every step, let Jesus be your vision. Keep the vision of what you were created for, and called to do, in front of you. It is so important to have a vision for your life-giving direction to living — and then to actually live it! The Lord will bring fruit in your life.

Follow Jesus in response to His call to "...Follow me..." (John 1:43). This is your call and privilege as His girl! As you follow Him, He will lead you into knowing and experiencing more of Himself and His plans for you. It is so freeing! What is so amazing is that this leads you to the personal relationship with Him that you were created for — staying dependent on, and being led by His Spirit, in line with His Word, and not just getting locked into following a plan.

Take the next step with Jesus in surrender. Take the next step with Him that He is calling you to take in this moment. Ask Him, "What next, Jesus?" What has He shown you to do? Take that next step. Sometimes He gives you a long-term view of where He is calling you, and sometimes He shows you only the next step!

If you are not sure what the next step is, you can simply look at His Word, the Bible, and see what He has called you to do and apply one of those things to your life.

To get you started, here are some ideas from Bible verses:

"…You shall love the Lord your God with all your heart and with all your soul and with all your mind and with all your strength." (Mark 12:30)

"…Encourage one another and build one another up, just as you are doing." (1 Thessalonians 5:11)

"Go therefore and make disciples of all nations…" (Matthew 28:19)

What is Jesus asking you to do to follow Him today?

_____

_____

_____

Stay surrendered in His hands. Look to Jesus and say, "I will do anything, Jesus." and then follow where He leads – day by day, moment by moment, for your whole life! Trust and leave the pen in His hands. Choose to follow Him instead of your feelings and desires. And find out for yourself the goodness of His ways!

Embrace Jesus and what He has for you right now. As we looked at before, every step of your life story is an invitation to go more deeply into Jesus and all He has for you in knowing, growing in, and shining Him. Walk with Jesus and receive fully what He has for you in this moment, day, and season. Do not miss what He has for you right now by being distracted with what might be ahead in the future. Focusing on who you know Him to be, what He is teaching you, and what He is doing in you now is preparation for what He has ahead!

Seek to lift Jesus up in every life season. Show His goodness right where you are – whether you are in the middle of schoolwork, facing a long-term illness, or anything else. In the place He has you, seek to experience and shine to the world that – "Jesus is good and He is enough."

Watch the story He unfolds. As you follow Him step by step, you will have the thrill of watching Him unfold His unique story for your life!

Which of these ways of embracing your story for His glory would be especially helpful for you right now?

Living for an Audience of One — A Powerful Help in Living Your Jesus Story

Have you ever been in a big crowd? Think of an Olympic event, and the crowd gathered to watch. When an Olympian is competing for the gold medal, does it matter if that person is pleasing the crowd? Or, does it only matter if that person pleases the judges? What matters is that they please the judges to win the gold medal, right?

Let's say there are people in the crowd with all kinds of opinions and perspectives – some cheering and some booing. What would you think if the crowd started shouting for the Olympian to do certain things that were against the competition rules? Suppose the Olympian chose to listen and respond to the crowd and became disqualified from receiving the gold medal. Would the Olympian be saying at the end, "I am so glad that I made the crowd happy!"? No way! That would be so silly, wouldn't it?

Listen so closely, friend. You live with your own "crowds" in your life – different people and groups who have opinions and ideas of what you should do. These include people in social circles, at church, at school, etc.

Write some of the "crowds" in your life here.

_____

_____

All of your life, people are going to be giving you their opinions of you, your choices, and what they think you should be doing. If you listen to them, you will be pulled in a million different ways. When you try to please multiple people out of fear of them, or a desire for their approval, it will lead you into bondage and lots of stress!

It is so paralyzing living to please others. *"The fear of man lays a snare, but whoever trusts in the LORD is safe."* (Proverbs 29:25) It is freeing to listen to and follow Jesus alone! He is the only One it matters if you listen to and follow. (Of course, it is wise to listen to counsel from those who will echo His voice.) Live for Jesus alone – and not for others and what they think you should do! If the crowds in your life are cheering or booing or silent, it doesn't matter.

I like to think of this as living for an "Audience of One." When you are living for Jesus – your Audience of One – it will change your life and lead you into everything that is right. Galatians 1:10 says, *"For am I now seeking the approval of man, or of God? Or am I trying to please man? If I were still trying to please man, I would not be a servant of Christ."* Are you being a servant to other people's opinions and being held in bondage to that? Or, are you living just for Jesus? This has been one of the most freeing things for me!

Live for Jesus alone.

Throughout my life, I have already had so many different "crowds" trying to influence me with their suggestions and ideas for what I should do with my life. When I listened to the people and lived for their praise, I ended up exhausted and confused. But when

I listened to Jesus, there was so much freedom, joy, and peace. I am so grateful for every time that I followed Jesus' will.

Let me be clear. The Lord is already pleased with you in Jesus! This is your secure position in Jesus – in His pleasure, love, and acceptance – that you cannot earn or lose as His girl. As you rest in and live from, that secure place of His pleasure in you in Jesus, you have the delight to follow and obey Him out of love and gratitude. And as you do, you bring joy to His heart! So listen to Him tell you how loved and accepted you are in Jesus – and go live from that position! Out of love for Him, seek to follow what He has called you to and bring joy to His heart!

When you are looking to the Lord, saying, "All that matters is what You think. What does Your Word say about this? What do You want me to do?" it is going to give you such freedom, peace, satisfaction, security, and fulfillment. It is so amazing to be able to get to the end of the day and say, "Jesus, as I get to the end of this day, all that matters is what You think." Live listening to Jesus, following Him, and ignoring what others say or think. In this moment, at the end of the day, and at the end of your life, you will be so glad for all of the times you listened to and lived for Jesus alone! As you live for Jesus as your "Audience of One," it will give you the freedom to seek, live for, and follow Him like you never could otherwise.

Challenges You Will Face

Like a hiker preparing for a long journey over a variety of terrain, it is important to be realistic that there will be hard times, resistance, and challenges in this life story on earth. Your story will include joys and trials, laughter, and tears. It will not always be easy – in fact, it can sometimes be very hard. But it is always worth it, both now and in eternity.

Jesus said, "I have said these things to you, that in me you may have peace. In the world you will have tribulation. But take heart; I *have overcome the world."* (John 16:33) Remember that Jesus is the hero of every part of your story! Depend on Jesus and keep your eyes focused on Him and the reality of your story in Him. This is why you are alive, is the greatest life you can live, and it is what matters now and in eternity. It will help you to walk through the challenges in your story with Jesus, by the power of the Holy Spirit!

Yes, there will be hard times – but it is so worth it. It is the only path worth living, and where you are only truly alive spiritually. He is with you, working in it for your good. Again, you have this amazing promise: *"…All things work together for good…"* (Romans 8:28)

Let's look at some of the challenges you may face in your story:

The enemy – the devil – wants to stop you from living in the Lord's amazing story for you. *"Be sober-minded; be watchful. Your adversary the devil prowls around like a roaring lion, seeking someone to devour."* (1 Peter 5:8)

There will be spiritual battles. You are in a spiritual battle, Jesus has the victory, and the enemy will not finally win. *"Fight the good fight of the faith. Take hold of the eternal life to which you were called and about which you made the good confession in the presence of many witnesses."* (1 Timothy 6:12)

You may think the story is about you, but Jesus can help you remember the Truth and walk in the joy of it being about Him. *"…That in everything he might be preeminent."* (Colossians 1:18)

There will be times when you feel weak, weary, and discouraged. *"…Let us not grow weary of doing good, for in due season we will reap, if we do not give up."* (Galatians 6:9)

You might be tempted to settle for less. *"Enter by the narrow gate. For the gate is wide and the way is easy that leads to destruction, and those who enter by it are many. For the gate is narrow and the way is hard that leads to life, and those who find it are few."* (Matthew 7:13-14) You are like a mountain climber, knowing the journey is hard, but so worth it!

You may have times where you cannot feel Him there – though He is always there. Listen to this, friend – Jesus is right there with you every moment of your life. When you are crying all alone, He is there. When you can barely contain yourself with joy, He is there. When you are facing a struggle with sin, He is there. When you are soaking in His Word, He is there. When you are faithfully living your everyday daily life, He is there. He has promised this, *"…I will never leave you nor forsake you."* (Hebrews 13:5)

You will struggle and fall. The times you struggle and fall are a place where you can experience the beauty of His grace to you. His grace empowers you to obey, and His grace is there to pick you up when you fall. *"…The righteous man falls seven times and rises again…"* (Proverbs 24:16)

Jesus will be with you through every step of life as you face these challenges, and He will give you the grace to overcome them! By His Spirit at work in you in these challenges, He can turn the struggles you face into places where you see the Lord's mighty work in your story! The beautiful thing is to remember that you are His, He loves you, He is working for His greatest glory and your best, He is always with you, and you are in His hands forever. Remember that the story ends in victory, with you being with Him in Heaven for all eternity. No matter what you face in your story, it is so worth it!

Listen to this beautiful promise from Isaiah 43:1-7: *"…Says the Lord… 'Fear not, for I have redeemed you; I have called you by name, you are mine. When you pass through the waters, I will be with you; and through the rivers, they shall not overwhelm you; when you walk through fire you shall not be burned, and the flame shall not consume you. For I am the Lord your God, the Holy One of Israel, your Savior…you are precious in my eyes, and honored, and I love you… Fear not, for I am with you…everyone who is called by my name… whom I created for my glory, whom I formed and made.'"* Isn't this a comfort?

It is a Journey of Faith

Yes, it is a journey of following Jesus in faith. It is meant to take you deeper into your relationship with Jesus and His Word and to grow your faith in Him. *"...We walk by faith, not by sight."* (2 Corinthians 5:7) If it is easy to see, it does not require faith, right? You do not need to know the whole story of your life. You only need to know Jesus – and know that He has the whole story written out! As you simply answer His call to, *"...Follow me."* (Luke 5:27), in each step of life, He will then lead you into all that He has for you.

The longer you walk with Jesus, the more you can look back and see His hand in your life. Just as you develop a history and a deep trust with a good friend over time, it is even more so with Jesus. As you walk with Him and experience new opportunities to trust Him, your faith will grow. It is so incredible. You will see glimpses now of the story He is writing – and it will leave you in awe. Like someone pulling back the curtain to a beautiful display and giving you just a glimpse of the beauty, someday, in Heaven, you will see the big picture and be blown away, in awe of the beauty of His plan.

Follow Him in faith and see what He will do!

Now you are called to walk with Him by faith. Follow Him in faith and see what He will do! As you follow Jesus in surrender and faith, He will take you on the most incredible journey – writing the most incredible story – beyond what you could imagine! It is a journey of faith! *"Trust in the LORD with all your heart, and do not lean on your own understanding. In all your ways acknowledge him, and he will make straight your paths."* (Proverbs 3:5-6)

Journaling the Journey — A Powerful Tool

Have you ever kept a journal? A journal is where you write down things that are happening in your heart and life. Journaling can be a powerful way to process, identify what the Lord is doing in your heart and life, and have a record for the days to come. (It also helps you to be able to share with others what He is doing in your life!)

Questions to ask as you journal your journey with Jesus:

- What is Jesus doing in my life?
- What is Jesus teaching me right now?
- What is He calling me to do today?

What you write can be simple, like – "I am learning that I can trust Jesus," "Jesus is opening a door for me to serve at church," etc. It can also be more in-depth, where you pour out your heart, share what He is doing, record a special Bible verse, and more.

It is not so much how you do it, but that when you do it, it helps you stop and reflect on what Jesus is doing in this part of your journey. Keeping a journal can be an incredible blessing! I would encourage you to start a journal of your journey with Jesus. You can grab a notebook, or a special journal, and a pen – or even keep a journal digitally. It will be a rich tool in your growth journey with Him – and a treasure to have for years to come! *"I will recount the steadfast love of the Lord, the praises of the Lord, according to all that the Lord has granted us..."* (Isaiah 63:7)

Comforting Realities in Every Season and Chapter

In every season of your life and chapter of your story, these beautiful truths are the same, filling you with faith, comfort, and confidence!

- Jesus is the same. *"Jesus Christ is the same yesterday and today and forever."* (Hebrews 13:8)

⫸ He is always with you. *"…He has said, 'I will never leave you nor forsake you.'"* (Hebrews 13:4)

⫸ He is for you. *"If God is for us, who can be against us?"* (Romans 8:31)

⫸ He is working for His glory and your good. *"And we know that for those who love God all things work together for good, for those who are called according to his purpose."* (Romans 8:28)

⫸ He is keeping you. *"I give them eternal life, and they will never perish, and no one will snatch them out of my hand."* (John 10:28)

⫸ and more!

Isn't that comforting to rest in?

Practical Application Step

Grab a journal and answer these questions, or you can write your answers right here if you want!

What is Jesus doing in my life?

_____

_____

_____

_____

What is Jesus teaching me right now?

_____

_____

_____

What is He calling me to do today?

_____

_____

_____

You can make this a habit that you do every day, once a week, etc. – or whenever you feel it is helpful!

No Other Life Compares

Remember this: Jesus and this life in Him for His glory is your purpose! No other life compares. You walk this journey on earth with Jesus and with your eyes fixed on Him. Jesus is your treasure, Heaven is your home, eternal life is yours – you live for this! If this journey of life is filled with hard things, it is okay because it is not your home. You are promised eternal life in Heaven with Jesus that will be full of joy!

Your Jesus Story

Jesus is writing a story for His glory in your life. It is a transforming journey. Each step with Jesus of following Him can bring you closer to Jesus, grow you in Him, and lead you into His plan for you! You can long and seek for your story to lift Jesus up for His glory. "...Whom I created for my glory..." (Isaiah 43:7)

Go for a story that puts Jesus center stage and holds Him up like a diamond to the light, as the treasure He is, for all to see! You know how the story ends – with Jesus, victorious, and in Heaven – forever. You can view all of this earthly story in light of that reality. It is the truest "happily ever after" ever – for all of eternity! The one you were made for – that is better than any fairytale!

A Story for His Glory and a Journey with Jesus

Your story is a journey with Jesus. He is your story, the Author and Perfecter of your story, and the One within you who empowers you to live it with Him!

Listen to these beautiful verses from the Bible:

"Therefore, since we have so great a cloud of witnesses surrounding us, let us also lay aside every encumbrance and the sin which so easily entangles us, and let us run with endurance the race that is set before us, fixing our eyes on Jesus, the author and perfecter of faith, who for the joy set before Him endured the cross, despising the shame, and has sat down at the right hand of the throne of God. For consider Him who has endured such hostility by sinners against Himself, so that you will not grow weary and lose heart." (Hebrews 12:1-3)

Your life story is like a race. As you run your race with your eyes on Jesus – the Author and Perfecter of your faith – you can know He is with you every step. He is the One who made you His through faith and Who will continue to walk with you each step as you live this story for His glory! He began it, and He will complete it! Isn't that comfort and security? Jesus is with you every step – until you see Him face to face and are with Him forever. *"…I am with you always…"* (Matthew 28:20)

This is the most amazing adventure with Jesus as you live out the story that He has planned for you as a part of His big story! It is so exciting! Will you live out this story yourself? You have the joy to walk with Jesus and watch as He unfolds a story for His glory in your life! ⤳

STUDY GUIDE

What was one thing that was especially helpful to you in this chapter?

_____

_____

_____

What is one step that you will take today to apply it to your own life?

_____

_____

What is one struggle that you face in this area that you can ask Jesus to help you overcome?

_____

_____

Look up these Bible verses and write what Jesus shows you:

- Jeremiah 29:11

_____

_____

- Hebrews 12:1-3

_____

_____

_____

- 1 Corinthians 2:9

_____

_____

_____

Pray or write out a prayer of response to Jesus.

_____

_____

_____

_____

Write the Focus Statement for this chapter.

_____

_____

_____

_____

You can write any additional thoughts here.

_____

_____

_____

_____

focus statement

PERSONALLY GO
with Jesus
INTO THE WORLD
AND LIVE IN HIM
as His girl

CHAPTER 10

Your Personal Response

YOUR CALL TO PERSONALLY EXPERIENCE JESUS AND THE VIBRANT LIFE YOU WERE CREATED FOR IN HIM AS HIS GIRL

"…Who do you say that I am?" (Mark 8:29)

....

Is this life in Jesus as His girl real for you?

Oh friend, you want it to be!

This amazing life in Jesus must personally be yours for you to experience Him and live it for yourself. You must own it and it must be real to you. You must personally respond to Jesus' invitation to be His girl. If you come to Jesus – by personally responding to Jesus, trusting Him as your Savior, following Him as your Lord, and embracing the life that He has called you to – you will experience Jesus and the life you were created for in Him!

We have had an amazing journey together, friend! You have seen a glimpse of the life you were created for in Jesus as His girl, how to embrace it, and the fruit that will come if you do! It is so amazing! Now it all comes down to it being yours and you experiencing it personally. The essential thing is that it is real for you! Is it?

Let's review the vision statement:

> You were created to know Jesus and live a vibrant life in Him as His girl — a life where you are fulfilled in Him, thrive in your Christian walk, and shine Him for His glory!

Isn't that so inviting and beautiful?

Okay, pause. Now, insert your name here:

> _____ was created to know Jesus and live a vibrant life in Him as His girl — a life where I am fulfilled in Him, thrive in my Christian walk, and shine Him for His glory!

This is the time where you need to make sure that it is real for you personally! You were made for this. Whether or not you are His girl impacts your soul, life, and eternity. All your life with Him forever hinges on it. It is more important than anything in the world that it is real for you.

Let's look!

What a Personal Response Really Is

You have seen a glimpse of the wonder of Jesus and the amazing life you are called to in Him as His girl. You have seen a vision and elements of this life in Christ. It is now how you personally re-spond to His invitation – your response to Jesus and the life you are created for in Him as His girl. It is great to know about it and think it is wonderful, but it is only when you believe and receive it for your-self that it is yours. When it is yours, you experience the wonder of it for yourself, and your life is changed forever.

You want to experience it for yourself!

What if someone you love and trust offers you an opportunity to take a dream vacation? You can hear about the offer and think it is good and true. But you must personally believe the offer, receive it yourself, and go on that vacation for it to be real for you and for you to experience it for yourself! Do you see this? That is only a small thing compared to how your personal relationship with and life in Jesus will change your life and bring you joy.

Make sure that it is real for you personally!

This is a real-life walk of faith with your Je-sus as His girl that will impact every ounce of your being. It is taking Jesus at His Word, living in it, and experienc-ing it yourself!

It is Real — Let it be Real for You

This is real! Like we said before, this is not a fairytale or an un-realistic idea – this is what you were made for in Jesus from the beginning of time! I plead with you to make sure it is real for you! Nothing else truly matters in this life or eternity. Is it real for you? Where you can say – "I am Christ's, I know my Jesus, and I am expe-riencing this life in Him!" Stop and ask yourself – "Is it real for me? Is it something that I am believing, walking in, and experiencing for myself in a real way? Or, am I only hearing about it, knowing about it, and just acknowledging with my mind and mouth that it is good?" It is only real to you when you walk in it! Keep seeking until it is real in your life. And then go deeper for the rest of your life! You so want it to be real for you!

Remembering the Powerful Realities of Being His Girl

We have had such an amazing time looking at Jesus and this life in Him together!

Let's look back on each chapter! Write one thing you remember about each chapter in the space provided. It can be a main point, the focus statement, a Bible verse, or whatever the Lord used to encourage you!

1. Catching the Vision – the vibrant life you were created for in Jesus as His girl

_____

_____

_____

2. Becoming His Girl – what it means to be Christ's girl and why it matters more than anything that you are His

_____

_____

_____

3. Walking with Jesus in a Real Way – finding what your heart is longing for in Christ

_____

_____

4. Your True Identity – who you are because of Whose you are and how living in it changes your life

_____

_____

_____

5. A Girl of the Word – the transforming power of God's Word vs. feelings, thoughts, lies, and culture

_____

_____

_____

6. Growing in Jesus – the process of becoming like and radiating Jesus from the inside out

_____

_____

_____

7. Living as His Girl – authentically living as Christ's girl by the power of His life in you

_____

_____

_____

8. Serving and Sharing Jesus – serving the One Who has changed your life and sharing Him with a world who needs Him

---

---

9. Your Jesus Story – your unique life story for His glory as you follow Jesus

---

And, now we come to…

10. Your Personal Response – your call to personally experience Jesus and the vibrant life you were created for in Him as His girl

I hope this book is just the beginning of a journey with Jesus or an encouragement along the way with Him! It is only a glimpse – and not the full picture – of all He has for you. You will grow in understanding and experiencing more as you read the Bible and walk with Jesus. I long that this helps point you to Jesus, His Word, and the life you are created to live by His Spirit in you – and that you to continue to follow Jesus for the rest of your life. If you have Jesus, you have all you need.

It is Your Personal Response

It is your personal response to Jesus in becoming His girl. When you are His is when you will experience Him and the vibrant life you were created for in Him as His girl. You must believe, receive, and walk in it yourself. Step forward in faith. It is why you were created! You see, we could talk about this for pages and pages – and the rest of our lives. But, if it is not yours, it is of little value. It must be real to you. You must taste it for yourself – like the ice cream illustration we looked at before. *"...Taste and see that the Lord is good..."* (Psalm 34:8)

Again, your parents, friends, etc. cannot believe for you – it is your personal response!

Your response to Jesus' invitation to be His impacts your relationship with Jesus, your life here on earth, and your eternal destiny.

If you have Jesus, you have all you need.

Like the powerful question of Jesus, *"...who do you say that I am?"* (Mark 8:29), it is Who He is to you that makes the difference. Your life will flow from that. This is what you want to experience yourself, friend!

When you experience it, your life is forever changed! Do not stop until it is so real for you personally!

How You Walk in It

You can stop and tell Jesus your desire, "I want to know You and embrace the life that You created me to live in You for Your glory!"

Then, take His hand in faith and step forward to know, believe, receive, be transformed by, live in, and share Him. Place your faith in Jesus as your Savior and Lord. Follow Jesus as His girl, empowered by His Spirit and life in you, and experience for yourself the life you were created for in Jesus. *"For I, the LORD your God, hold your right hand; it is I who say to you, '...I am the one who helps you.'"* (Isaiah 41:13)

Look to Jesus and take the next step He guides you in today! If you are looking for a step to take – after making sure that you are His – look back over your study guide pages in this book and choose one of the things you wrote in the "One step I will take today to apply it" section.

What is one step you can take today?

_____

_____

_____

Every step taken towards Jesus, by the power of His life in you, is a step deeper into Jesus and the life you were created for in Him as His girl!

You can say for yourself, "I have known about this. Now I am living it! I am His, looking to Him, walking with Him in this life by His Spirit in me – and experiencing Jesus and the life I was made for in Him as His girl!" Your life will be transformed!

The Time is Now

The time to become His girl, to know Him, and to live the life you were created for in Him is now. Do not wait for tomorrow.

When I had tasted the Lord for Who He really is, He gave me such a passion to share Him with others – especially girls and young women. This led to lots of different, exciting opportunities to serve Him. I loved it, had a vision for it, and knew it was what I was meant to be doing.

There was a point in the process where I looked around and saw other young people my age spending time just hanging out and having fun, and I was tempted to think that I should possibly take it a little less seriously. (That's where the problem of comparison can get you!) I was allowing that thought to stay in my mind for a day or two.

Then one night, my dad brought home the newspaper with a front-page story about three girls from a Christian family who were in a car crash and killed. I will never forget looking at the front cover of the newspaper, seeing the picture of the youngest girl, and real-izing that she was one of the girls who had been at our first confer-ence for girls that past summer. I was so grateful to find out she was His! At that moment, what was truly important, came clearly into fo-cus. It showed me that all that matters is that you are His and all that will truly last is your relationship with Jesus and the souls of people!

Do you see how important it is?

This is what matters for you, for me, and for everyone!

"...Choose this day whom you will serve... as for me... will serve the LORD." (Joshua 24:15)

It Changes Your Life

In the pages of this book, you've seen a glimpse of how expe-riencing Jesus and a life in Him as His girl will transform your life! I hope you have caught a vision! You can live from a place of experi-encing Jesus and this life for yourself. It results in spiritual life, satis-faction, joy, purpose, and eternal hope. And, there is much more! It impacts every area of your life.

You can start today and then continue to discover more. As His girl, you can experience Him and these realities as your own every day, for the rest of your life on this earth. You can say, "I have ex-perienced Jesus and this life in Him that I was created for!" It will change – and continue to change – your life for as long as you live, until you see Jesus face to face.

Can you see a picture of what this could look like in your life? Isn't it so exciting? It is amazing beyond words! I so want you to experience this for yourself!

You cannot even begin to imagine what Jesus has in store for you! You will discover it more and more as you embrace Him and this life in Him and experience it for yourself. Once you truly experi-ence Jesus and this life in Him for yourself, you will find that nothing compares! *"...What no eye has seen, nor ear heard, nor the heart of man imagined, what God has prepared for those who love him..."* (1 Corinthians 2:9)

Do Not Let Anything Hold You Back

Friend, in these pages, we have discussed many things that can hold you back from Jesus and living as His girl. This time, we will look at the need for a personal response. What is potentially holding you back from becoming His girl or this vibrant life in Jesus? Stop and think about that. Is there anything? Do not let anything hold you back. Nothing is worth holding you back from why you were created!

All that matters now and in eternity is if you are His.

I want to say this with love and serious care for you – you can talk the talk, go to church, etc., but not truly know Jesus. I want you to know Him, be His, and experience life in Him now and for eternity. This is all that truly matters.

Someday, you will stand before Jesus. In that moment and for all of eternity, all that will truly matter is if you responded to the call to be His, and experienced Jesus and the life He created you to live in Him, personally. All that matters now – and will matter then and in eternity – is if you are His. Make sure that it is real for you – salvation in Him, relationship with and life in Him, and your eternity with Him as His girl! It must be personally yours.

What is holding you back? Things that can hold you back include:

≫ fear
≫ feeling like you have to have it all together
≫ and more.

What is it for you? You can acknowledge it in your heart, or write it here:

———————————————————————————————

———————————————————————————————

———————————————————————————————

Take a moment right now to give and release it to Jesus, and ask Him to remove it. You can tell Him, "I give it to You, Jesus." He wants all of you and your heart. He wants you to come to Him as you are, to become His, and to allow Him to make you into all that He created you to be. Don't wait until you have it all together – because you never will. It is only when you come to Jesus, and He does His transforming work in you, that you will be changed. Then, He will continue His beautiful work, for the rest of your life until you see Him face-to-face! *"...He who began a good work in you will bring it to completion at the day of Jesus Christ."* (Philippians 1:6)

Remember where your hope lies – Jesus.

Let it be real for you! Do not miss this! It is the reason you are created. Experience it for yourself. Let nothing stand in the way, by His grace. It is worth it, friend.

You Were Made for This

This is what you were made for in Jesus!

It is this personal life in Him as His girl where: Jesus is real to you. You are His girl. He is real in you, by His Holy Spirit. His Truth transforms your life. You are secure in your identity in Him. He is working in your heart and growing you. He is empowering you to live a vibrant life as His girl. His light is shining through you to the world around you for His glory. You will be with Him forever in Heaven.

Yes, friend, you were made for this. This call is before you. It is possible, a joy, and worth giving everything to experience it as yours!

Who is Jesus, and what is this life in Him as His girl, to you personally? It is only as real as it is when it is only you and Jesus. Do not stop until it is real for you personally!

Christ's girl is growing as a girl who knows:

>> why she is here
>> Whose she is
>> Who her Jesus is
>> who she is in Him
>> what is true
>> what she is called to do
>> and she lives in and from the reality of these truths by the power of His Spirit in her, for His glory. This results in glory for Jesus, joy for her, and blessing for others.

Jesus is calling girls in this generation who will walk with Jesus, experience His Truth for themselves, and shine Him to a world hungry for Jesus! Will you be one?

Call to Action

It comes to you, friend. Will you personally answer Jesus' call to be His girl and experience Him and the vibrant life He created you for in Him? Will you look to Jesus, believe, and walk as His girl by His grace and for His glory?

Jesus is calling you to it. He is giving you the grace to respond. It is a personal call that you must personally answer. Receive it for yourself! You can stop and tell Him, "Jesus, I want to be Your girl, to know You personally, to thrive in the life You created me for in You, and to shine you to the world for Your glory!"

He hears you, receives you, comes into your life, and this moment is the beginning of a journey that will continue for as long as you are here on this earth – until you see Him face to face and are with Him forever in eternity!

Application Step

Take a moment to pause and pray or to write out a prayer of response to Jesus.

If it is true, insert your name here:

"...You _____ are Christ's..."

(1 Corinthians 3:23)

Go Live as His Girl

Now, go live as His girl! This is why He made you! As you do, you will experience Jesus and the life you were created for in Him as His girl!

"...You are Christ's..." (1 Corinthians 3:23)

My prayer of response to Jesus:

A Prayer for You

As we close, know I have prayed this for you.
Jesus has amazing things in store!

Dear Lord,

You are amazing! Thank You for all that You are, for the gift of being Yours, and for all that You have in store for us in You! You are life!

Thank You for the girl reading this book and for who You are calling her to be as Your girl, the life You created her for in You, and the power of Your Spirit in her.

I pray that she would:

>> *catch the vision*
>> *be Yours*
>> *know You*
>> *love You*
>> *grow and thrive in You*
>> *stand on Your Word*
>> *walk in her identity in You*
>> *live as Your girl*
>> *follow You*
>> *shine You for Your glory*
>>   *— personally.*

Jesus, You are amazing, life in You is vibrant, and Your call and what You have in store for her is amazing! I pray that she would not settle for less than You, Your call, and all that You have for her life in You.

"For this reason I bow my knees before the Father, from whom every family in heaven and on earth is named, that according to the riches of his glory he may grant you to be strengthened with power through his Spirit in your inner being, so that Christ may dwell in your hearts through faith—that you, being rooted and grounded in love, may have strength to comprehend with all the saints what is the breadth and length and height and depth, and to know the love of Christ that surpasses knowledge, that you may be filled with all the fullness of God. Now to him who is able to do far more abundantly than all that we ask or think, according to the power at work within us, to him be glory in the church and in Christ Jesus throughout all generations, forever and ever. Amen." (Ephesians 3:17-21)

We love You, Jesus, and look forward to all that You will do!

In Your name we pray, Jesus,

Amen.

Starting a Book Study

You can start a *Christ's Girl* book study for more encouragement and fellowship in living vibrantly in Christ as His girl! It can be so special and powerful to go through this book with others. Know that it can be a powerful time of seeking Jesus with others who desire to know, love, and obey Him. It can be a great blessing to you and them! Here are some ideas:

You could study this book with...

⇒ Someone one-on-one (a friend, a mentor, your mom, a younger girl you are mentoring, etc.)
⇒ A group of friends
⇒ A group of younger girls you are mentoring
⇒ A mother and daughter group
⇒ A group of girls at church, a small group, or a group of girls you want to reach for Jesus
⇒ And more!

Ideas for Your Time Together

⇒ **Book content** – You could read each chapter and fill in the blanks ahead of time, and then review the content together as a group, followed by discussion and prayer time. You could read the chapter together, take time to fill in the blanks, followed by discussion and prayer time. Or, you could read the chapter and fill in the blanks ahead of time, read the chapter again as a group, followed by discussion about what you read and prayer time.

≫ **Discussion time** — You could use the provided chapter study guides to guide your discussion time or could come up with your own discussion questions.

≫ **Prayer Time** — You can have prayer time as a group, or break up into pairs to pray.

Sample Outline of Your Time Together

This sample outline may be helpful, but you can arrange or plan the time however you desire!

≫ Welcome everyone (you can do an icebreaker game or sing).

≫ Review the material, or read the chapter, together.

≫ Discuss the material, look up the Bible verses, share testimonies about the topic, and pray together.

A couple of optional things:

≫ Do a craft to go with what you are studying.

≫ Share a snack and fellowship.

You are free to study this book however Jesus leads you! These are a few ideas. He has great things in store for you. May the Lord richly bless you as you seek to know, love, and follow Him — and encourage others to do the same!

> *"...What no eye has seen, nor ear heard, nor the heart of man imagined, what God has prepared for those who love him..."*
> (1 Corinthians 2:9)

For Continued Encouragement

It has been such a joy to seek Jesus together with you in these pages! You can visit us for more encouragement in Jesus and living the vibrant life in Him you were created for as His girl at:

www.christsgirlministries.org

We would love to cheer you on in Jesus and continue the journey with Him together!

Acknowledgements

I am so grateful to everyone who played a role in this book!

Most of all, to my Jesus – You are my Savior, my All, my Life. Thank You for bringing me to Yourself, for saving me, and for this fulfilling life in You. I long for this book to be used by You to bring many girls to see how wonderful You are.

To my amazing husband, Brian – You are a priceless gift to me from Jesus. Thank you for loving me like Jesus loves His Church, for being my wonderful husband, and for all of your encouragement with this book! I am so grateful to be your wife.

To my sweet baby girl – How sweet to find out that you were on the way in the midst of writing this book. May you be Christ's girl and experience Jesus and the life you were created for in Him as His girl! You are so loved.

To Dad and Mom – You have been my cheerleaders from day one. You have walked genuinely with Jesus before me, loved me, invested so much in encouraging me in Him, and supported His call on my life. I am so grateful the Lord blessed me with such amazing parents!

To all of my little sisters in Jesus – who I love so much, are such a gift to my heart, and fill me with joy as I watch you walk with Jesus, live vibrantly in Him, and shine Him to the world around you. I am cheering for you!

To the amazing team that made this book a reality:

Dad — for your incredible proof editing of the manuscript and encouraging me in the Lord's call on my life.

The proofing team — Bria, Cara, Carlie, Grace, Heather, Ingretta, Jenny, Kathy, Kimmie, Lianna, Sally, Sharie, and Stacy. You were amazing in helping this book become better. I am so grateful for your insights and friendship!

Rebecca Radicchi — for being my editor who has prayerfully edited this book to make it better.

Ruth Gulbranson — for your precious friendship and all of your editing wisdom.

Annie Wesche — for your friendship, love for our Jesus, and your prayerful dedication to excellence in style in designing the book cover for His glory.

Sarah Bryant — for your loving investment in the layout design of this book and for being a dear sister.

Pastor Brent Nelson — for your faithful theological editing of this book and for being a faithful pastor.

To all who prayed for the book, cheered me on, talked over ideas, offered insight, and so much more.

To all who have had such a beautiful part in my life, the girls' ministry, and this book — who are too many to mention. Jesus knows who you are and you are a gift.

To you who are reading this book — I am so blessed by your heart to experience Jesus and the vibrant life you were created for in Him! I hope to see you someday as His girls all gather in Heaven with our Jesus and worship Him forever!

I am so grateful!

Personal Notes

Made in the USA
Monee, IL
14 December 2022